125 — top 127. (unemployment)
132 – 3   Kathy Sinnott
153 – 4 Kerry Roads.
155 –   Bosman Rule
158 – .161. – ↙

185 . Fair Trade

Impact!

Civic, Social and Political Education for Junior Certificate

Impact!

Civic, Social and Political Education
for Junior Certificate

3RD EDITION

Jeanne Barrett and Fiona Richardson

GILL & MACMILLAN

Gill & Macmillan Ltd
Hume Avenue
Park West
Dublin 12
with associated companies throughout the world
www.gillmacmillan.ie

0-7171-3522-5

Design and typesetting by Anú Design, Tara
Illustrations by Karen Allsopp
Additional illustrations by Design Image
Colour Repro by Typeform Repro Ltd.

*The paper used in this book is made from the wood pulp of managed forests.
For every tree felled, at least one tree is planted, thereby renewing natural resources.*

Contents

Acknowledgments   viii

About CSPE   ix

CHAPTER 1

Section A – The Individual   2

Study 1	A New Beginning	2
Study 2	Bullying	4
Study 3	Our Needs and Rights	8
Study 4	Discrimination	12
Study 5	Rights Across the Globe	17
Study 6	Taking Responsibility	22
Study 7	The Family	25
Study 8	Changing Conflict	27

Section B – The Environment   31

Study 9	Think Globally – Act Locally	31
Study 10	Acting Locally – Thinking Globally	37
Study 11	So What Can You Do?	40
Study 12	Action Project Ideas	44
Study 13	Revision Questions	46

CHAPTER 2

Section A – Your Community   52

Study 14	What is a Community?	52
Study 15	Local Government	53
Study 16	Interview with a Councillor	57
Study 17	The Wasteland	60
Study 18	A Local Environmental Officer	63

Section B – Communities in Action		66
Study 19	Case Studies – Communities Taking Action	66
Study 20	Do It Yourself!	72
Study 21	Ideas for Action Projects	75
Study 22	Revision Questions	76

CHAPTER 3

Section A – Our State		84
Study 23	Democracy and You	84
Study 24	Your Vote – Use It	88
Study 25	Political Parties	89
Study 26	Interview with a Member of the Green Party	92
Study 27	How Ireland is Governed	95
Study 28	Dáil na nÓg	100
Study 29	A Day in the Life of an Taoiseach	102
Study 30	An Tánaiste, An Interview	104
Study 31	An Independent TD Speaks	106
Study 32	An Interview with a Senator	108
Study 33	Making Law	110
Study 34	The Law	112
Study 35	Influencing the Government	119

Section B – The State and You		124
Study 36	Case Studies – In Action with the State	124
Study 37	Ideas for Action Projects	134
Study 38	Revision Questions	135

CHAPTER 4

Section A – Ireland and the World		140
Study 39	Our Connections to the EU	140
Study 40	The History of the EU	143
Study 41	The EU – How It Works	146

Study 42	EU Budget – EU Funds	149
Study 43	Ireland and Issues in the EU	151
Study 44	How You Can Influence the EU	153
Study 45	Interview with an MEP	156
Study 46	The United Nations	157
Study 47	The Irish Defence Forces and the UN	162

Section B – Developing Our World — 165

Study 48	Child Labour	165
Study 49	The Debt Crisis	169
Study 50	The Arms Trade	174
Study 51	Refugees	177
Study 52	Know Racism	182
Study 53	Fair Trade and Ethical Trade	184
Study 54	Non-Government Organisations	188
Study 55	Ideas for Action Projects	194
Study 56	Revision Questions	195

CHAPTER 5

Assessment for CSPE — 202

Study 57	Action Projects and Skills	202
Study 58	Your Guide through a RAP and CWAB	216
Study 59	Revision for Written Exam	231
Appendix:	Useful Addresses, E-mails and Websites	247
	Picture Credits	254

Acknowledgments

The authors would like to acknowledge the help and advice given by the following:

Amnesty International, Focus Ireland, Pavee Point, the Council for People with Disabilities, Ann Carroll, Department of the Environment, Department of Justice and Law Reform, Department of An Taoiseach, *The Irish Times*, the *Wexford Echo*, *The Clare Champion*, the *Irish Independent*, Garda Martin Gibbons and Garda Derek Dempsey, Gaisce – The President's Award, Guinness Living Dublin Awards, Environmental Endeavour Awards, The Green Party, Fianna Fáil, Fine Gael, The Labour Party, The Progressive Democrats, Olywen Enright TD, Sinn Féin, The Socialist Party, Marian Harkin TD, ALONE, ISPCA, Combat Poverty, DEFY, ACTIONAID, ARASI, Brian Ruane, Annette Honan and Clare O'Neill of Trócaire, A.F.r.I., Ballymun Partnership, Billy Lewis of Moy Valley Resources, The Burren Action Group, Fair Trade Network, World Development Movement, National Youth Council of Ireland, Concern Worldwide, Offices of the European Parliament, Mary Banotti, the UN High Commission for Refugees (Ireland), Sorcha Kelly, Captain Tom Clonan, Private John Kelly, Brian Crowley MEP, Kathy Sinnott, Know Racism Campaign, National Children's Office, ENFO, News Four, An Taisce, Richard Maguire of Galway City Council, Ballygowan ECO Awards, Councillor John Ryan, Sadhbh O'Neill, Kilkenny County Council, the *Irish Examiner*, Linda Noary, *Southside People News*, URBAN Ballyfermot, the Vincentian Partnership for Social Justice, Tánaiste Mary Harney, The Equality Authority, Detective Garda Cathal Delaney, East Timor Ireland Solidarity Campaign, Oran Doyle, Ireland Aid, Citizen Traveller, Barnardos, ENFO, News Four, Senator David Norris, Goal, The Irish Red Cross, Trust, Trevor Sargent TD, Aengus Carroll, Pat Cox MEP, Mary Keane, Eva Richardson McGea, Meagen Barrett.

For permission to reproduce extracts, the authors are grateful to the following:
Adrian Mitchell for his poem, 'Back in the Playground Blues'; Richard Rogers for 'Case Study on Curitiba, Brazil', adapted from *Cities for a Small Planet*, Richard Rogers (ed) and Phillip Gumuchdjian (Faber & Faber, London 1977); 'Changing Times at the Security Council' (United Nations), adapted from articles in *Newsweek*, January 2000; Jacqueline Wilson and Nick Sharratt for *Dustbin Baby* (Doubleday, 2001).

The authors extend their thanks to the teachers and students of Killinarden Community School, Tallaght and Loreto College, St Stephen's Green.

The authors would like to dedicate this book to their families.

About CSPE

Civic, Social and Political Education (CSPE) is about considering what it means to be an **active citizen**. It is a course based on human rights and social responsibility. You will find out about the part you can play in all the **communities** that you are a member of:

- family community
- school community
- local community
- national community
- world community.

The CSPE course is divided into **four main units** of work.

The Wider World – unit 4

Ireland – The State – unit 3

The Community – unit 2

The Individual & Citizenship – unit 1

This book is divided in the same way:
- the individual is looked at in chapter 1
- the community is the topic of chapter 2
- Ireland – the State is discussed in chapter 3
- the wider world is the focus of chapter 4.

Each chapter in this book looks at the way people take part in these communities and the different issues, concerns and difficulties that people are interested in.

CSPE also looks at **seven key concepts** or ideas. Each chapter and study in this book is related to one or more of these concepts. The seven concepts are:

- **Rights and Responsibilities** – You will learn about human rights and how rights go hand in hand with responsibilities.

- **Human Dignity** – You will learn whether people are valued and respected in Ireland and throughout the world. You will see how basic needs like food, health and education are vital to human dignity.

- **Stewardship** – You will learn how we are all stewards of the planet and how we can be responsible citizens of the planet through our actions.

- **Development** – You will learn how development can be a way of improving the communities we are a member of, and also how development may cause difficulties when rights clash.

- **Democracy** – You will learn about democracy and how we can all take a part in the way the country is run.

- **Law** – You will learn about the importance of rules and laws and how laws are a way of making sure that the rights of people are protected. Laws are also about protecting life and property. You will also discover how rules and laws are used to bring about a peaceful end to conflicts or differences.

- **Interdependence** – You will learn how we all depend on each other and how our actions as individuals, e.g. what we buy, can have an effect or impact on situations and places we have never seen.

Through your Junior Certificate exam in CSPE you will show your understanding of these seven key concepts. You will also show your understanding of the concepts and units by doing an action project.

What is an Action Project?

'An action project actively involves the students in undertaking tasks which extend the development of an issue or topic beyond the usual limits of textbooks and course materials.'

(Taken from DES Guidelines for Schools)

CSPE is concerned with you being an active citizen. It is through your action project that you show how you can take action over an issue that concerns and interests you. In **chapter 5** you will find details of how to go about doing an action project. Before doing an action project make sure you read this chapter.

When you decide to take action on an issue that concerns you, remember the following points.

- The action project should be clearly **based on one or more of the seven concepts** that the CSPE course looks at.
- The action project should have a **human rights and social responsibility angle**.
- The action project should involve an **action element**. Look at chapter 5 for more information on the different actions you could do. At the end of each chapter there are many ideas for action projects.
- The action project should involve you **contacting and engaging with other people** and communities on the topic or issue.
- The action project should allow you to **develop skills**. See chapter 5 for more information on skills.
- The action project should help you to **develop your knowledge and understanding** of the subject or topic of the action.
- Each student must write their own **individual report** on an action.

When you have taken part in an action project, the next step is to write it up for your Junior Certificate exam. You write the details and findings of your action project in either a **Report on an Action Project (RAP)** or in a **Coursework Assessment Book (CWAB)**.

The marks for your CSPE Junior Certificate examination are awarded as follows:
Report on an Action Project (RAP) 60%
or
Coursework Assessment Book (CWAB) 60%
Written Exam 40%

Remember: You will find **steps to an action projects** and the **skills** involved in action projects as well a guide to **doing a RAP and a CWAB** in chapter 5. At the end of each chapter you will also find **exam-style revision questions**.

The Impact! Workbook, which is also available separately,
is packed with a variety of extra activities.

01 chapter

SECTION A – THE INDIVIDUAL   **SECTION B** – THE ENVIRONMENT

FOCUS
IRELAND

SECTION A The Individual

Civic, Social and Political Education looks at what it means to be a citizen and how each of us can participate in the various groupings or communities we are members of. We are all members of a family community, a school community, a local community, as well as a national community and a world community. Being a member of a community means that we have certain rights but it also means that we have duties and responsibilities to the other people in that community.

Study 1 A New Beginning

You are now a member of a new school, a new community. There are different rules and responsibilities that are part of being a member of this community. Understanding these new **responsibilities** and seeing why there are rules can help you in your new surroundings.

Read the diary and see if you have anything in common with Phil.

Monday, 3 September

Dear Diary,

Well today was my first day in secondary school. All the new first years got brought into the hall and then were divided into their classes. The teachers all looked a bit serious. My first class was with my class tutor who told us what was expected of us, but more to the point, what was not expected of us! He made us take out our journals and he went through all the rules and regulations. I don't understand why some of the rules are there.

Tuesday, 4 September

Dear Diary,

Got lost a few times. Some of the older students are nice but others just jeer at the

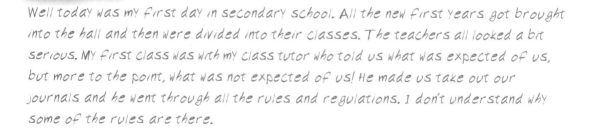

First years. Leaving Cert. students came into class today to tell us about the clubs and sports that we can join. I think I'll join the basketball club. One of the other students in my class got caught sticking gum under her desk. The teacher went mad saying how unfair it was to expect others to clean up after you. My classmate has to write out the school rules tonight.

Wednesday, 5 September

Dear Diary,

Had my first Science class. We all put on white coats and goggles to do an experiment. I enjoyed doing that but I'm not too sure I understand exactly what the teacher was talking about. I hope I won't find this subject too hard.

Thursday, 6 September

Dear Diary,

I'm getting to know more of the names of my classmates. One or two of them slag others a bit and have made up some mean nicknames. One of my classmates got upset when they started slagging her. I hope they stay away from me.

Friday, 7 September

Dear Diary,

The weekend is here! All in all I've had a pretty good week. I think this place is going to be OK. I really enjoyed woodwork today and French was a laugh. Our tutor told us about the school council today. We have to elect two members from our class to the school council. The election will happen around mid-term. She told us the council was a place where students could have a say in the running of the school. I think I might be interested in this because I'd like all first years to have their own lockers. My bag is so heavy with all these new books!

⚙ Activities

1. Phil's tutor got the class to go through the school rules. Phil is not sure why some school rules are there. Look at the rules below and give reasons for them.

   a No chewing gum.

   b Arrive to school on time.

   c No running in the corridor.

   d Have respect and consideration for all members of the school community.

   e Come to class properly prepared.

   f Do not damage school property.

2. One of Phil's classmates was being called names. What would you do in this situation?

3. If you were the class rep on the school council, what would you talk about that concerns first years?

4. There are certain things you could do to make sure that life in school is enjoyable or difficult. Here are some examples:

ENJOYABLE	DIFFICULT
Join lots of school clubs.	Miss school for no reason.
Help a friend who found Irish hard.	Claim you couldn't do your homework because you fell in love.

ACTION

Research: Find out about all the clubs and teams that you can join in your school. You could make a list of all these clubs and teams and give them out to the other first year classes.

Study ❷ Bullying

Many schools have a rule that states that 'all members of the school should treat each other with respect'.

Pupils have the right to come to school and feel safe and secure, have friends and be able to learn and have fun. Bullying is a situation where a person is not treated with respect, where school is no longer enjoyable or a place where they feel safe and secure.

'. . . The playground was three miles long
and the playground was five miles wide
It was broken black tarmac with a high fence all around
Broken black dusty tarmac with
a high fence running all around
And it had a special name to it, they called it
The Killing Ground.

Got a mother and a father,
they're a thousand miles away
The Rulers of the Killing Ground are coming out to play
Everyone thinking: who they going to play with today
. . . You get it for being Jewish
Get it for being black
Get it for being chicken
Get it for fighting back
You get it for being big and fat
Get it for being small
Oh those who get it and get it
For any damn thing at all . . .'

(Taken from Back in the Playground Blues
by Adrian Mitchell)

 Activities

1. In the poem *Back in the Playground Blues,* how does the young person show that they are afraid of the playground?

2. Why does the person in the poem feel that their mother and father are 'a thousand miles away'?

Bullying can take many forms.

Physical

⊕   Hitting, punching, kicking, threatening, taking or hiding belongings.

Verbal

⊕   Insulting, name-calling, nasty or racist remarks, repeatedly teasing.

Indirect

⊕   Spreading nasty rumours, leaving a person out of a group on purpose.

Bullying is a behaviour which is hurtful and done on purpose and which lasts for weeks, months or even years. It is often very difficult for those being bullied to defend themselves. People do not have a right to hurt others.

Bullying behaviour can affect a person in many ways.

⊕   They are unhappy or afraid to come to school.

⊕   They feel their lives are miserable.

⊕   They can find it difficult to concentrate and learn.

⊕   They can be injured.

⊕   Some people can get stomachaches and headaches, and have nightmares.

> '. . . It became a part of their routine
> To take his money and make him scream
> To twist his arm and bash his head
> "If you tell Sir, that's it! You're dead!" . . .'

(Taken from The Victim *by Ann Carroll)*

 Activities

3.   In the poem 'The Victim', why do you think the bullies' behaviour is allowed to continue?

4.   Who could you report a bullying incident to in your school?
   - Class prefect
   - Tutor

- A teacher you get on well with
- Principal
- A class representative
- Year head
- Other

A lot of bullying incidents are witnessed by other pupils. However, many incidents of bullying are never reported. Often there is an unwritten rule that there is something wrong with 'ratting'. If you do nothing when you see someone being bullied, the bullies may think that you approve of what they are doing. Many students who are usually kind and caring may behave in a horrible way because it makes them feel part of a group. If you are aware of bullying in your class you can choose to do something about it, and not be a bystander.

You can:

- Refuse to join in.
- Be friendly to the person being bullied.
- Persuade the student to talk to a person that they trust, e.g. older student/teacher/parent/relative.
- Offer to go with the student to speak to someone who can help.
- Bring the situation to the attention of the school council if your school has one.
- Make sure the student is not left out of groups.
- Report the bullying behaviour yourself to a teacher.

We all have needs – in order to survive we need food, water and shelter. We also have a right to these things, just like every person has the right to love, friendship and to feel safe and secure.

Activities

5. Pupils who are being bullied are sometimes afraid to tell anyone about what is happening. What signs can parents and teachers watch out for in pupils who might be being bullied?
6. If you became aware of someone being bullied, what could you do to help?
   Hints: hang out with them at break time/walk home with them.
7. The government is worried about bullying and wants to reduce it. You are in an advertising agency that has been asked to design an awareness campaign ➡

about bullying. In groups, discuss your ideas for the campaign. You could:

- make posters
- make badges
- make leaflets
- make up a slogan or logo
- carry out a survey or questionnaire (example of survey p. 209).

8. Many schools, offices and other places of work have anti-bullying charters or codes. Does your school have an anti-bullying charter or list of rights for the people in your school? Design a charter, including five to six statements or points on how people should be treated. For example: no one should gang up on another student.

Study ❸ Our Needs and Rights

The needs and rights of people are protected when individuals, communities and countries take responsibility for safeguarding them. Rights are concerned with the freedoms and respect that should be given to all people. It was because of the loss of human life and the suffering caused by World War II that the **United Nations Organisation** came into being. In 1948 the countries that joined the United Nations put together a list of rights which they believe every human being is entitled to. This list of rights, or charter, is called the **United Nations Declaration of Human Rights**. The UNDHR is not a legal document as such, but rather more a statement of how people should treat each other. Below is a summary of the charter.

- *Everyone is born free and equal.*
- *Everyone has the right to food, clothing and housing.*
- *Everyone has the right to work, health and education and has duties to the community.*
- *Everyone is equal before the law and has the right to its protection.*
- *Everyone has the right to equal treatment before the courts.*
- *Everyone has the right to rest and leisure.*
- *Everyone has the right to marry.*
- *Everyone has the right to freedom of thought, conscience and religion.*
- *Everyone has the right to a nationality.*

human dignity

- Everyone has the right to own property.
- Everyone has the right to take part in the government of his/her country.
- No one should be subjected to torture or slavery.
- Everyone has the right to asylum in other countries to escape from persecution.
- Everyone has the right to freedom of opinion and expression.

In many cases these rights have yet to be achieved. Abuses of human rights still happen in many places throughout the world today.

In 1959 the **United Nations Convention on the Rights of the Child** was drawn up. A convention is a more legally binding agreement. Ireland signed this convention in 1990, and it was ratified in 1992. 'To ratify' or 'ratification' is to make a more legally binding promise, so Ireland has made a legally binding promise to uphold the rights laid out in the UN Convention. Below is a summary of the Convention.

- Children have the right to enough food and clean water.
- Children have the right to be with their family or those who will care for them.
- Children have the right to health care.
- Children have the right to an adequate standard of living.
- Children have the right to special care and training.
- Children have the right to play.
- Children have the right to free education.
- Children have the right to speak their own language and practice their own religion.

- *Children have the right to be kept safe and not be hurt, exploited or neglected.*
- *Children must not be used as cheap labour or soldiers.*
- *Children have the right to protection from cruelty, neglect and injustice.*
- *Children have the right to express their own opinions and to meet together to express their views.*

The Convention on the Rights of the Child has been signed by most countries around the world, with the exception of the USA and Somalia. The USA has difficulties with Article 37 of the Convention, which states that 'children have the right not to be subjected to torture or degrading treatment. If detained, not to be kept with adults, sentenced to death, nor imprisoned for life without the possibility of release'. As the USA operates the death penalty this article caused a problem for them.

Activities

1. Choose *five* rights from the Declaration of Human Rights or the UN Convention on the Rights of the Child and rank them in order of importance. Give reasons for your choices.
2. Draw up a Charter of Rights for *one* or more of the following groups: parents/teachers/students.

   OR

   Draw up a Charter of Rights for one of the groups above and compare the rights you have suggested with those of your classmates, and reach an agreement (consensus) on at least five rights.

Right on Our Doorstep

The first article of the UN Declaration of Human Rights says, **'Everyone is born free and equal'**, yet many people are not treated equally. They are unable to join in, or fully take part in, society. In our society different groupings of people feel that they do not have equal rights. These groups could include people who are homeless, people with disabilities and people living in poverty. Here is an example of some of the rights that these groups might be denied.

People who do not have equal rights	Rights included in the UN declaration
The homeless	Right to housing
People with disabilities	Right to work
People living in poverty	Right to food and clothing

People with Disabilities

For many people being able to go to work or school, enjoy sports, have a family and social life, read a book, go to the cinema, drive a car or hop on a bus are things they don't think about. But for 360,000 Irish citizens any or all of the above may cause problems; that is because 360,000 people, or ten per cent of the population, have a disability. People with disabilities may experience particular problems trying to get equal rights as citizens in society.

They may experience inequality in terms of:
- access (being able to get into buildings)
- using transport
- education
- getting suitable housing or accommodation
- finding work.

Yet it is the right of every Irish citizen to have these things. As one person with a disability said:

'People with disabilities do not want to be pitied nor do they want their disabilities to be dismissed as of little importance. All that is required is a little respect and basic needs and rights. Surely this is not too much to ask?'

(from a summary of the Report of the Commission on the Status of People with Disabilities)

A survey carried out by the Irish Wheelchair Association showed that:
- 87.5% of their members are not in open employment
- 74% are not in education or training programmes
- 50% are not involved in normal social activities outside the home
- 27% believe that their accommodation is totally unsuitable for their needs.

Activities

1. Look at the survey by the Irish Wheelchair Association. Can you suggest reasons why many of their members are not involved in education and training programmes, employment and normal social activities?
2. How well does your school meet the needs of people with disabilities?
3. Make a list of the changes that would have to be made in your school so that a wheelchair user, a blind person or someone who uses crutches could fully participate in school life.
4. Name other groups in society whose rights may be denied.
5. Who do you think is responsible for making sure that everyone has equal rights?
6. What rights are being denied to the people in these pictures?

ACTION

Poster: Design a poster about one or more of the rights contained in the UN Convention on the Rights of the Child.

Study ④ Discrimination

If a majority of people in society label a certain group or community as being bad, dirty, stupid or worthless, blame them when things go wrong in society or give them no help to improve their situation, such action is called **discrimination**.

human dignity

Within Irish society there are different groups that feel they are discriminated against. There are also many organisations that concern themselves with the rights of certain groups, raising awareness of their situation and helping them. For example, Focus Ireland and the Simon Community concern themselves with the needs and rights of people who are homeless. ALONE is concerned with the needs and rights of the elderly, while the **Irish Society for the Prevention of Cruelty to Children** is concerned with the rights and needs of children.

Homelessness
Focus Ireland

Focus Ireland believes that 'everyone has a right to a place that they can call home'. It provides a wide range of services for people who are homeless, such as emergency and short-term residential units as well as providing long-term accommodation for its customers in Dublin, Limerick and Waterford.

Being homeless means:
- not having a place of privacy or a place to keep things that are important to you
- not having anywhere to cook or store food
- not having a place of shelter
- not having your own bedclothes or furniture
- if you have children it means not having anywhere for them to play or to feel safe and secure.

Focus Ireland Housing Advice Centre

Focus Ireland estimates that:
- there are 3,000–5,000 homeless adults in Ireland at any one time
- about fifty per cent of people who use their services are under twenty-five years of age.

Activities

1. Are you surprised to learn that fifty per cent of the people who use the services of Focus Ireland are under twenty-five years old? Explain your answer.
2. Write a short story imagining what your life might be like as a person who is without a home.

Stereotype!

People or groups within society are often discriminated against because of **stereotyping** and **prejudice**. Stereotyping can be positive or negative. An example of a negative stereotype is to say that all Irish people drink too much, or all women are better than men at minding children.

Prejudice means to prejudge a person or group. It is having a view of a person or group without having met them. This is often based on stereotyping.

Activities

1. Explain what discrimination means in your own words.
2. Name other groups in society that are often stereotyped and describe the stereotyping.
   Hints: teenagers/football fans/teachers.
3. Explain how stereotyping might lead to a person or group being treated badly.

The Travelling Community

The Travelling community is a group within Irish society that feels discriminated against and that feels that their needs and rights are not being met.

The following is a story of one Irish Traveller.

'I remember when we were doing the summer project for the Traveller children and we decided to go to a fun factory. When we got there we were told it was only for booked groups, so we left. This settled woman who was with the group rang up and asked for a booking, but she didn't mention that we were Travellers. When we arrived back their eyes nearly popped out of their heads and this woman said, "It's bookings only." She didn't know what to say when we told her we had booked.

So anyway, all the kids lined up, including one settled child who was with the Traveller children and the woman pinpointed her and said, "Come over here. You're not allowed with them." The little one said, "Yes, I'm with this group." The woman didn't know what to say.

I was brought up in the country and I never heard the word 'knacker' until I came to the city. I said to my father, "What's a knacker?" He said, "That's an old horse that's ready to go to the slaughterhouse." "Why do they call me that?" I said. "I don't know," said my father. You hear people say about Travellers: "Look at their jewellery. Look at their vans." Their jewellery is their bank. If they get short of money they take it to the pawn shop and get it back when they can afford it. The Travellers need vans to make their living. It's just the same as settled people. Some have good jobs and others have bad jobs. Some Travellers have a good way of living and others have a bad way. Travellers are often not served in pubs or shops. I know there are rowdies, but there are rowdy settled people and they're rarely banned. There is too much discrimination against Travellers these days.'

The Traveller community have experienced discrimination in Ireland

Pavee Point, an organisation that concerns itself with the needs and rights of Travellers, estimates that:

- there are approximately 24,000 Travellers in Ireland.

15

Research has also shown:

- ❋ only two per cent are sixty-five years of age or over
- ❋ forty-eight per cent had no piped water
- ❋ fifty per cent had no toilet
- ❋ fifty-four per cent had no access to public electricity.

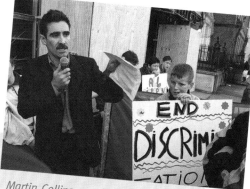

Martin Collins speaking against discrimination

🜚 Activities

1. How would you feel if you were one of the children on the trip to the fun factory?
2. Why do you think that Travellers are sometimes refused entry to shops and other places?
3. Why do you think that only two per cent of Travellers live beyond the age of sixty-five?
4. Why do you think that the placing of halting sites within settled communities can cause problems?
5. The fears and worries that both the Travelling community and the settled community speak about are real. Both communities are concerned with their rights. Can you suggest ways that would bring about a better understanding between both communities?

(From the Citizen Traveller Poster Campaign.)

CITIZEN TRAVELLER

Champion Sprinter
Daughter
Singer **Traveller**
Show-off
Best Friend
Citizen

It's time to value Travellers as people with their own culture, needs and contribution.

Travellers halting site

Good accommodation for Travellers means good neighbourhoods.

CITIZEN TRAVELLER

6. What do you think these posters are saying?

Study 5 Rights Across the Globe

Amnesty International is a worldwide movement of people who campaign for human rights. British lawyer Peter Benenson launched the organisation in 1961 after reading about two Portuguese students who had been sentenced to seven years in prison for raising their glasses in a toast to freedom. At the time, Portugal was run by a military dictatorship.

Today Amnesty has over one million members in over 140 countries and territories. There are also over 3,500 youth and student groups worldwide including 150 groups in schools across the Republic of Ireland. Its famous symbol of a candle surrounded by barbed wire was inspired by the Chinese proverb **'better to light one candle than to curse the darkness'**. As Peter Benenson himself put it:

> 'The candle burns not for us, but for all those whom we failed to rescue from prison, who were shot on the way to prison, who were tortured, who were kidnapped, who 'disappeared'. That's what the candle is for.'

The Amnesty symbol near the Customs House in Dublin

These words can be seen etched around the 'Eternal Flame' near the Customs House in Dublin city centre. They are also to be found on posters, T-shirts and postcards in dozens of languages all over the world. The candle is recognised everywhere as a symbol of **hope, justice and freedom**.

Amnesty International is not political. Its vision is of a world in which every person enjoys all of the human rights written in the Universal Declaration of Human Rights and other international human rights documents.

The Aims of Amnesty

Amnesty has two main aims:

1. **To promote general awareness of human rights, such as:**
   promoting awareness of the values contained in the Universal Declaration of Human Rights and other internationally agreed human rights standards encouraging the acceptance that human rights must be protected.

2. **To oppose specific abuses of human rights, such as:**
   - torture and other cruel or inhuman treatment and excessive use of force for all prisoners
   - the death penalty
   - the imprisonment of people who have not used violence, because of their beliefs, ethnic origins, sex or colour
   - executions and disappearances.

Amnesty also opposes:
   - children taking part in armed conflict
   - the return of refugees to countries where they may be at risk of serious abuses
   - the sale of arms (including weapons and training) to countries where it is likely that these may add to human rights abuses.

Amnesty is Changing

Amnesty members have always worked on behalf of people in other countries. They can now also act on issues which affect the countries in which they live. For example, Amnesty members in Ireland have recently worked to raise awareness of **racism** and have campaigned for fair treatment for asylum seekers and refugees. In the future, Amnesty will also work harder to help the millions of people around the world who are denied other rights, such as the right to food and the right to education.

The Power of the Pen

Amnesty's main weapons are letter writing, lobbying and raising awareness. One of the ways Amnesty brings **human rights abuses** to the attention of governments is through letter writing. Amnesty members and supporters write to governments, prison officials, other people of influence and sometimes prisoners themselves. It puts pressure on those holding prisoners and gives hope and comfort to those being held. It has helped in the release of prisoners and in the improvement of their conditions.

Amnesty often receives letters from those who have been released. Here are some of their comments:

'When the first 200 letters came, the guards gave me back my clothes. Then the next 200 came, and the prison director came to see me. When the next pile of letters arrived, the director got in touch with his superior. The letters kept coming and coming: three thousand of them. The president was informed. The letters still kept *arriving and the president called the prison and told them to let me go.'*

Former prisoner of conscience from the Dominican Republic.

We could always tell when international protests were taking place ... the food rations increased and the beatings were fewer. Letters from abroad were translated and passed around from cell to cell; but when the letters stopped, the dirty food and repression started again.'

Former prisoner of conscience from Vietnam.

'Your efforts saved my life.'

Former prisoner of conscience from South Korea.

'Your kindness and ongoing support saved me from the executioner.'

Former death row prisoner from the USA.

Activities

1. Why did Peter Beneson set up Amnesty International?
2. How many Amnesty youth and student groups are there in Ireland?
3. What is the famous symbol of Amnesty International?
4. What is Amnesty's vision of the world?
5. Can you name two human rights abuses that Amnesty opposes?
6. How is Amnesty changing?
7. What work does Amnesty say that they will work harder at in the future?
8. What are Amnesty's main weapons in their work to stop human rights abuses around the world?
9. How is it shown in the text above that Amnesty's campaigns have worked?

Read the following case study from Amnesty Ireland.

Take Action!
Take a step to stamp out torture.

> Firoz was only nine years old when the Bangladeshi police allegedly tortured him. They thought he had stolen a mobile phone. Now aged ten, he took ten months to recover from the terrible physical injuries inflicted upon him and is

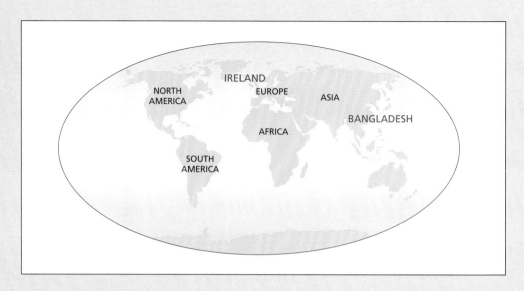

still receiving treatment to help him recover from the mental trauma he suffered.

Firoz and his father were helping a family to move house in July 1999 when the phone went missing. While Firoz's father was away moving things from their house for them, the family accused the boy of stealing their phone, which he denied. According to Firoz they were just about to let him go when their twenty-five-year-old son took him away from the others and began to beat him. 'He kept slapping me on the face and punching me on the shoulder, and then he got hold of a stick and was just about to hit me on my head. I thought he was going to kill me so I began to scream. Then a neighbour, who knew my father, came to the house and told the man to stop beating me, so he let go of me.' His father returned to the house, protested about the beating and took Firoz home.

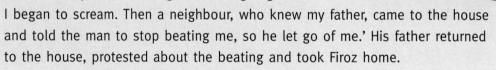

That night at around three am, the police came to the house and arrested Firoz. He said they began to beat him in the house. They restrained him in such a way that it made breathing difficult for him. 'They kept asking me where the mobile was and when I told them that I had not seen it, they slapped and beat me.' Firoz was then taken to the police station where they made him squat on the floor. A policeman applied such heavy pressure to Firoz's bent knee that it was injured. They left him overnight in a cell, and the following morning they treated him so badly that his hand was seriously damaged ➡

human dignity

and he passed out. Firoz's family were not allowed to see him while he was being detained. Eventually, his father managed to get a letter from a local politician requesting the officer in charge to release him. His father was made to sign a blank piece of paper – with his thumbprint because he cannot read or write. Firoz's family have decided not to file any complaints against the police because of fear of revenge from the police.

Although Firoz's case was taken up by human rights activists, the government has failed to carry out an investigation or bring those policeman responsible for the torture to justice.

Join Amnesty's campaign by writing a letter urging the Bangladeshi government to investigate allegations that Firoz was tortured and bring the people responsible to justice.

Activities

1. Why was Firoz arrested by the Bangladeshi police?
2. What kind of treatment did he receive in jail?
3. From the Declaration of Human Rights and the Convention on the Rights of the Child, can you say what rights Firoz was denied?
4. How did Firoz's father get him released from jail?
5. Why didn't Firoz's family file a complaint against the police?
6. What does Amnesty International want the Bangladeshi government to do about this case?
7. Why would Amnesty International want you to take action in a case like this?

ACTION

Guest Speaker: If there is an Amnesty group in your school invite one of the members to give a talk to your class on Amnesty's work.

Research: Find out about Amnesty's latest campaign by visiting their website – www.amnesty.ie. You could produce an information leaflet on the campaign and give it to other students in your school.

Study 6 Taking Responsibility

Pastor Niemöller

Pastor Niemöller talks about what can happen when people do not look out for the rights of others. **Rights and responsibilities go hand in hand.** We all have the responsibility to look out for the rights of others. In doing so we are also protecting our own rights. If you don't speak out for the rights of others, who will speak out for you?

One person who spoke out against the denial of human rights in his country was Nelson Mandela.

Nelson Mandela (1918-)

Nelson Mandela was born the son of a tribal chief in Eastern Cape Province in South Africa. He became a lawyer and in 1944 joined the ANC (African National Congress), which was a non-violent civil rights movement. It promoted the interests of black Africans who were not, for example, allowed to become MPs or own more than thirteen per cent of the land of South Africa, despite making up seventy-five per cent of the population.

In 1948 the white minority government introduced a policy of **apartheid** (the word means 'separateness' in the Afrikaans language), designed to create strict racial division. The apartheid laws stated where black Africans could live, what kind of jobs they could have and where they could study. The laws created separate facilities for black and white people, such as separate toilets, and 'white only' sections on beaches. Marriages between black and white people were banned.

Many people joined the campaign to free Nelson Mandela

In 1960 the government banned all black political organisations, including the ANC. For the next thirty years it operated as an underground organisation. In 1961 the ANC formed a military wing (Spear of the Nation) and started a campaign against the government. In 1962 Mandela was sentenced to life imprisonment for being involved in ANC activities.

Nelson Mandela was to spend the next twenty-seven years in prison. During this time he became a hero to many millions of people because he stood for the triumph of

dignity and hope over despair and hatred. People in different countries showed their support by refusing to buy South African goods. In Ireland, for example, Dunnes Stores workers refused to handle any produce from South Africa.

Eventually, in 1990 Nelson Mandela was released from prison and the new South African

Mandela has said, 'A nation should not be judged by how it treats its highest citizens, but its lowest ones — and South Africa treated its imprisoned African citizens like animals.'

government, led by FW de Klerk, lifted the ban on the ANC. In the same year de Klerk ended the apartheid system.

In 1993 Nelson Mandela and FW de Klerk were awarded the Nobel Peace Prize for their efforts to bring about equality between all South Africans. In 1994 the first elections in which blacks were allowed to vote took place. Nelson Mandela became the president of South Africa.

On the day that he became president, Mandela talked about his struggle and what he called 'the long road to freedom'. He said:

'I have walked that long walk to freedom. But I discovered that after climbing a great hill, one only finds that there are many more hills to climb. I have taken a moment here to rest, to steal a view of the glorious vista that surrounds me, to look back on the distance I have come. But I can rest only for a moment, for with freedom comes responsibilities, and I dare not linger, for my long walk is not yet ended.'

Nelson Mandela as president of South Africa

Most people will not suffer like Nelson Mandela. He spent twenty-seven years in prison for speaking out against the denial of human rights. However, taking responsibility can be difficult even in our everyday lives. But whatever decisions we make, even doing nothing, means that there are consequences or outcomes to that decision.

Activities

1. How did the apartheid system affect the lives of the citizens of South Africa who were not white?
2. Why was the apartheid system a denial of human rights as set down in the UNDHR (United Nations Declaration of Human Rights, p. 8)?
3. Why did Nelson Mandela and FW de Klerk win the Nobel Peace Prize?
4. What do you think Mandela meant when he said, 'with freedom comes responsibilities'?
5. The following situation is a dilemma that you could be faced with in your life. Here are some of the possible choices and outcomes of a decision that you might make. ➔

You see a person being hassled by a gang at a street corner. Do you . . . ?

Possible Choices:	Possible Consequences:
(a) Phone the gardaí.	(i) You could be called as a witness.
(b) Do nothing.	(ii) The gang will escape and the victim could be injured.
(c) Try to help the person yourself.	(iii) You could be hurt.

Look at the following situation and decide what the possible outcomes or consequences could be for each of the choices given.

You are at a local club with your best friend. Someone you know offers you both drugs. Your friend decides to take them. Do you . . . ?

Possible Choices	Possible Consequences
(a) Say no and leave.	?
(b) Tell your parents later what happened.	?
(c) Take some yourself.	?
(d) Tell the bouncers what has been going on.	?

6. Make up your own dilemma, suggesting possible choices and consequences.
7. Write a short drama sketch based on a dilemma. This could then be acted out in class.

Study ⑦ The Family

The family is one of the most common **communities** in society. Being a member of a family sometimes means that we become involved in arguments and conflicts. These conflict situations can come about from simple differences over what TV programme to watch, what time you should be home by or who your friends should be.

'I wanted a mobile!' I wail like a baby.

'Oh for God's sake, April,' says Marion. 'You know perfectly well what I think about mobiles. I hate them.'

'I don't!'

'They're an absolutely outrageous invention – those ridiculous little tunes tinkling everywhere, and idiots announcing "Hello, I'm on the train" – as if anyone cares!'

'I care. I want to keep in touch with my friends.'

'Don't be silly. You see them every day.'

'Cathy is always sending text messages to Hannah and she sends them back, and they're always laughing away together and I'm always left out – because I haven't a mobile.'

'Well, that's tough, April. You'll just have to learn to live without it. I've told you . . .'

'Oh yeah, you've told me all right.'

'Please don't talk in that silly sulky tone, it's incredibly irritating.'

'I can't help it if you think I'm irritating. I don't see that it's so terrible to want a mobile phone when it's what every single teenager in the entire world owns without question.'

'Don't be ridiculous.'

'Why is it so ridiculous? I just want to be like my friends. Cathy's got a mobile. Hannah's got a mobile. Why can't I have a mobile?'

'I've just told you why.'

'Yes, well, I'm sick of you telling me this and telling me that . . .'

(Taken from Dustbin Baby *by Jacqueline Wilson)*

Activities

1. What is the cause of the conflict in this house?
2. What arguments does April use to get across her reasons for wanting a mobile?
3. What do you think of the way April reacts to her stepmum, Marion, when she says she can't have a mobile?
4. If you were April how would you have dealt with the disagreement?
5. What do you think of the way Marion deals with the disagreement?
6. Give examples of other family situations that can cause conflict.

rights and responsibilities

Drama: Do a role-play based on a typical family disagreement where compromise is used as a solution.

Study 8 Changing Conflict

There are many conflict situations throughout the world that have given rise to the denial and abuse of human rights. This has happened in countries such as Kosovo, Burma, Sierra Leone, Angola, Somalia and Rwanda.

In Northern Ireland the Good Friday Agreement is an example of a **compromise**, where Unionists and Nationalists tried to find a peaceful solution to their differences and disagreements.

Northern Ireland — The Good Friday Agreement

The long-standing religious and political conflict can be dated back to the plantations of the seventeenth century. The separate state of Northern Ireland was created in 1920. This state is part of the United Kingdom.

Those who want to continue the link with the UK are called Unionists. The majority of these are Protestants. Those who want to be linked with the Republic of Ireland are called Nationalists. The majority of these are Catholics.

Loyalist mural

Back in 1968 the Catholic community, which was in the minority, felt that their rights were not being met, e.g. their rights to jobs and housing. They started to march for equal rights. The conflict between the two communities increased as both sides believed that their culture, their religion and their way of life were being threatened. Some Republicans and some Loyalists took up arms believing they were fighting for the rights of their communities. This

Republican mural

27

resulted in many people being killed and others being forced to leave their homes. Since the beginning of this period, known as the 'Troubles', 300 children have lost their lives and thousands have been left without a parent.

Over the years many attempts have been made to solve the conflict. Finally, in 1995 a Framework for Agreement Document suggested new ways of dealing with the problem. It was decided to bring in people from outside Northern Ireland who were not directly linked with either community, such as Senator George Mitchell from the United States and General John de Chastelain from Canada. These people could talk to the Unionist and Nationalist parties separately, acting as independent chairpersons.

Together — David Trimble, Bono and John Hume

This led in 1996 to the **Mitchell Principles**, which said that only those political parties that agreed to solve the conflict by peaceful means could take part in the talks.

An agreement was finally reached on Good Friday, 10 April 1998. Its aim was to end the conflict by both communities working together and solving their problems in the new Northern Ireland Assembly.

During his speech announcing the Good Friday Agreement, Senator Mitchell said, 'It doesn't take courage to shoot a policeman in the back of the head or to murder an unarmed taxi driver.' He said that what takes courage is to use the tools of 'persuasion, fairness and common decency . . . to help build up this society instead of tearing it apart.'

A sign seen in Belfast showing that some people did not want to give up arms

The agreement was reached by all sides sitting down together and using debate and discussion as the tools of **persuasion** rather than bullets.

Issues such as the handing over of arms (decommissioning) caused problems between the two traditions, which resulted in difficulties in setting up the Northern Ireland Assembly.

Outbreaks of violence have occurred throughout this process as the two communities continue to find a way to live together in peace.

⚙️ Activities

1. What happened in 1968?
2. How can bringing in someone who is not involved in a conflict help solve it?
3. What are the Mitchell Principles?
4. What problem has caused the most difficulty?
5. In order to reach an agreement what did all sides have to do?
6. Why do you think that outbreaks of violence still happen from time to time?

At the beginning of the Troubles in Northern Ireland in 1968, Catholics started marching for rights they believed they were being denied. The idea came from the civil rights marches by black people in the USA, whose leader was Martin Luther King. He believed in solving a conflict situation by peaceful means only.

Martin Luther King (1929-68)

Martin Luther King was born in the USA in Atlanta, Georgia in 1929. He became a Baptist minister like his father. When he was studying in college he read about Mahatma Gandhi and was impressed with his ideas of **non-violent protest**.

In America during the 1950s there were many laws that were unfair to black people. They had to sit in separate parts of restaurants and at the back of buses, and they even had to give up their seats on buses if a white person wanted to sit down.

Martin Luther King

One day a black woman named Rosa Parks refused to give up her seat on a bus for a white person. Martin Luther King organised a campaign where all black people refused to get on any public buses in Montgomery, Alabama. They walked to work instead.

After 381 days, during which time Martin Luther King was put in prison, a new law was declared allowing black people to sit in any part of a bus they wanted. Neither did they have to get up to let a white person sit down.

Black communities marching for their rights in the 1960s

Martin Luther King went on to lead many **peaceful campaigns** to get better education and housing for black people. In 1963 he led a demonstration of nearly 500,000 people for better rights for black people in front of the White House in Washington. He made a famous speech where he said:

> *'I have a dream that one day the State of Mississippi will be transformed into an oasis of freedom and justice. I have a dream that my four little children one day will live in a nation where they will not be judged by the colour of their skin . . . when all of God's children, black and white, Jews and gentiles, Protestants and Catholics, will be able to join hands . . . '*

Martin Luther King continued to campaign peacefully for black people's rights until he was assassinated in 1968.

 Activities

1. What rights did Martin Luther King campaign for?
2. What was the main message of the speech Martin Luther King gave outside the White House?
3. Name some other people who have campaigned peacefully for rights.

human dignity

SECTION **B** The Environment

As individuals born on the planet we are the temporary owners or stewards of the earth. We are entrusted with its care and maintenance. All of us can play our part. All of us are capable of making a difference, of leaving the planet with its resources intact, ready for those who will be its stewards after us.

Study **9** Think Globally – Act Locally

Everything we do, from turning on a light switch to eating a hamburger, has an **environmental impact** somewhere else in the world. So how can each of us make choices that have a positive impact on our planet?

What is the size and impact of your global footprint? How can you make it smaller?

Energy Conservation

Our modern world depends on energy to keep it going. In Ireland the main sources of energy are coal, gas, oil, peat and water. Coal, gas and oil are **non-renewable** sources of energy. This means that one day they will run out. It is estimated that the world's supply of oil will run out by the end of this century.

But how can we help to conserve the energy sources we use at the moment? Energy used in the home accounts for thirty-five per cent of the energy consumed in Ireland.

We can all contribute to conserving energy at home by:
- switching off lights, computers, CD players or televisions when not needed
- insulating the attic
- sealing doors, windows and other gaps against draughts
- using energy-saving light bulbs
- when boiling the kettle, using only the amount of water that is needed.

Water Conservation

No life on earth could exist without water. Making sure that water supplies are clean is another means by which we can be responsible stewards of the planet.

Sewage from towns and cities, slurry and chemical fertilisers from farms and industrial waste from factories all find their way into our rivers and seas. This pollution causes algae and bacteria to grow, and these use up the oxygen fish need to survive. Toxic waste poisons marine life as well as causing illness in humans.

Water quality and **conservation** should be of concern to us all. Each of us can make our own water conservation efforts by:
- mending leaking taps
- taking a shower instead of a bath
- using the washing machine and dishwasher only when full
- not leaving the water running while brushing our teeth.

Getting Greener

You can become a better citizen and be more green by following the ten steps to a better environment.

stewardship

You can be a better citizen and be more green if you know your litter law. Under the Litter Pollution Act 1997, you are breaking the law when:

- **You** create litter in a public place.
- **You** put out your household rubbish for collection in a way that creates litter.
- **You** own or occupy land and you fail to keep it free of litter.
- **You** own or occupy land along a public road, in a speed limit area, and you fail to keep footpaths or grass verges along the road in front of your property free of litter.
- **You** own, hire or drive a car and litter is dropped from it.
- **You** fail to clean up if your dog fouls in certain public places, whether on the street, at a park, on the beach or – be warned – in the garden of another person's house.
- If you cause litter you can be faced with an on-the-spot fine of €125 or up to €1,900 in court.

(STEP 1)
Cut down on packaging!
It's easy | to make a difference.
10 easy steps to a better environment
1 Shop for the environment. Cut down on packaging. Buy goods and packaging that are made from recycled materials or are recyclable.
2 Do the right thing. Recycle.
3 Buy reusable shopping bags.
4 Compost your waste and get growing.
5 Don't Litter and don't tolerate those who do.
6 Water is life. Think about it and conserve.
7 Dispose of old paint and waste liquids properly. Don't pour them down the drain.
8 Leave the car at home from time to time.
9 Save energy. Use it sparingly.
10 Choose energy efficient labels A and B.
ENFO, Tel 1890 20 01 91.
Made from 100% Recycled paper
www.10steps.ie

You can be a better citizen and be more green by being concerned about what happens to all the waste we produce. The Irish Government produced a **waste management policy** in 1998 because of concern over our national waste problem. At that stage, ninety per cent of our rubbish was going to landfill sites (dumps) and only ten per cent of rubbish was being recycled. The landfill sites in Ireland were nearly full. There are also many other problems with landfill sites:

- they take up a lot of land
- dumps produce methane gas and this adds to the greenhouse effect
- they are a blot on the landscape.

Much of our waste goes to landfill sites that are now nearly full

In the past the rubbish that went to landfill sites was not sorted, but now every area (under the government directive) has to come up with a **waste management plan** for its own area. In the future it is hoped that waste will be dealt with in this way:

- 20% landfill
- 30% thermal treatment (this is where rubbish is burned but energy is also generated)
- 50% recycling.

Less Waste – Less Problems

Ireland produces twice as much household waste as it did fifteen years ago. We can reduce the amount of waste we produce by always thinking about this slogan:

REDUCE	REUSE	RECYCLE

The following diagram shows one way that we can cut down on the waste we produce and be better stewards of the planet.

PREVENTION

Prevention is the key to avoiding waste. Less waste means wiser use of our natural resources like coal, oil and peat. Much waste can be avoided at the purchase stage – Do you need to buy that product or service? Buy only the amount you will use. Do you need all the packaging?

MINIMISATION

Prevention is followed by minimisation. Think of where you can maintain, repair, share, or sell on. Buy goods that have a long life, for example long life batteries.

RE-USE

When you buy something can the product or packaging be reused? Go for refillable or reusable containers like glass bottles etc.

RECYCLING

Recycling is the next best. Try to choose products which are made from recycled materials, like copies made from recycled paper.

ENERGY RECOVERY

This is where energy is made when waste is disposed of in a particular way like thermal treatment. The energy made can be used to produce electricity etc.

DISPOSAL

This is the last option and is where we dispose of waste, for example in landfill sites etc.

rights and responsibilities

Reduce What?

We can reduce waste by being concerned about the amount of packaging we use.

- Bring your own reusable bag to the supermarket.
- Some packaging has to do with hygiene and protecting a product from damage. However, a lot of packaging has to do with making the product attractive to buy. Think about the Christmas presents and Easter eggs you buy and all the packaging that they involve.
- Buy products with packaging that can be recycled.

Think about how much unnecessary packaging is used on products you buy

Reuse What?

How many products can you reuse?

- Lots of household items can be reused for their original purpose, e.g. milk bottles and beer bottles, or used as containers for other things.
- Clothes can be reused by sending them on to a charity shop or using them as cloths.
- Reuseable cloth nappies cut down on the use of natural resources and water.
- Old newspapers can be used to mop up spills, etc.

Recycle What?

Think of all the things that can be recycled.

- **Paper** – newspapers, magazines, cardboard boxes, computer printouts, posters, telephone books, etc.
- **Glass** – all kinds of glass can be recycled, e.g. jars, soft drink bottles, beer bottles, wine bottles, etc.
- **Metals** – all aluminum cans can be recycled. All soft drink cans are made from aluminum. Many towns and neighbourhoods now have bottle banks and facilities where all of the above can be recycled.
- **Clothes** – old clothes and fabric can be recycled. Recycled cloth can be used as wiping rags in factories, made into new fabric like some tweeds or used to stuff furniture or cushions for chairs and sofas. Oxfam in England runs the largest centre for recycling clothes in Europe.

Recycling cuts down on the amount of waste we produce

A Community Recycles!

The environmental dimension of the regeneration of Ballymun swung into action last week when environmental consultant Trevor Graham travelled from Malmo, Sweden to join the north Dublin residents in launching their community recycling and composting projects.

In what seems like a model scheme, the projects include a composting machine, which will produce high-quality garden compost four to six weeks after householders deposit their kitchen waste (including fish and meat, which are usually excluded from compost bins because of the risk of attracting vermin).

Situated in a converted lift shaft under the Ballymun flats, the Swedish composting machine is the first of its kind in Ireland. A 'bring centre' is also up and running in the basement of a block of flats. There are sixteen householders involved in a pilot project which tells them how much waste they have diverted from landfill. So far, thousands of plastic bottles and drinks cans have been deposited, as well as hundreds of glass bottles, plastic shopping bags, food tins and paper bags. A bounty hunters competition for seven- to ten-year-old children resulted in more than 2,000 bottles and cans being collected. 'Accessibility is the key to getting people to recycle,' says Pat Turner, a Ballymun resident who is leading the project. 'People don't have to think twice about recycling when there's a facility on their doorstep open in the evenings and at the weekends. We hope to inspire other communities to set up similar recycling initiatives . . .'

(Taken from The Irish Times, *Horizon Report)*

 Activities

1. Can you think of ways that you could use less electricity?
2. Make a list of the different ways you use water in a day. Don't forget to include activities where you use water for leisure and relaxation, e.g. swimming.
3. Can you think of other ways you could conserve water?
4. Suggest ways you could reduce the amount of water (both at home and at school) which is used once and then thrown down the drain.
5. What ways can we recycle the following items: clothes, books, toys, furniture, plastic and organic waste?

6. Where is your nearest bottle and paper bank?
7. What are the effects of litter pollution?
8. How would you solve the national litter problem?
9. How would you go about running an anti-litter campaign?
10. What machine is in a converted lift shaft under the Ballymun flats?
11. What does the pilot project tell the householders involved in this scheme?
12. How were children included in the project?
13. What do you think of this project? Give reasons for your answer.

Study 10 Acting Locally - Thinking Globally

Many environmental problems are now of a global nature.
These include:

- global warming
- ozone layer depletion
- acid rain
- deforestation
- nuclear pollution
- danger to wildlife.

Global Warming

■ **Cause:** Burning fossil fuels like coal, gas and oil give off carbon dioxide.
Carbon dioxide, methane gas, and chlorofluorocarbons (CFCs) are often called '**greenhouse gases**'.
Global warming happens when heat from the sun gets trapped by these gases and cannot escape into the earth's atmosphere.

■ **Effect:** Global warming causes climate changes. Higher temperatures on the earth's surface causes the ice caps to melt. This in turn will cause sea levels to rise and flooding will occur. Small changes in temperature can have a huge effect. During the last Ice Age temperatures were only about 4°C lower than they are now. Some scientists think that the earth might get warmer by between 1.5°C and 4.5°C by the year 2020. Crop failure and drought because of changing rainfall patterns could be the result.

■ **Solution:** Green energy (or energy created by **renewable resources** like solar power, wind and water power) could be used more in industry and in our homes. In Ireland most of the energy is still created by burning fossil fuels. However, along with other EU countries we have agreed to create twelve per cent of our energy by renewable resources. Under the **Kyoto Agreement** – an international agreement to cut greenhouse gases – Ireland has agreed that in 2010 our greenhouse gases would be no more than thirteen per cent of the 1998 level. However, we have already gone over the level agreed and could face fines.

Ozone Layer Depletion

■ Cause: When we release man-made chemicals like CFCs into the earth's atmosphere they destroy the ozone layer, which is also in the atmosphere.

Smog caused by ozone depletion

■ Effect: Less ozone means more exposure to harmful ultraviolet sun rays that cause skin cancer. It can also lead to eye diseases, damaged crops, smog pollution and climate change.

■ Solution: Cut down on CFCs which are used in items like fridges, freezers, aerosols and glues.

Acid Rain

■ **Cause:** Acid rain is another result of burning **fossil fuels** (gas, coal, oil). Sulphuric and nitric acid in gases produced by power stations, factories and car exhausts dissolve in rain.

■ **Effect:** Acid rain damages trees, fish die in rivers and lakes and buildings are damaged. As the pollution agents can travel in the air the problems affect many countries. For example, half the acid rain that falls in Canada comes from the USA.

One result of acid rain is damage to monuments and buildings

■ **Solution:** Implement more pollution laws for power stations, factories and cars. Using renewable sources of energy like wind, solar and wave power will cut down on the amount of acid rain.

Deforestation

■ **Cause:** Trees are often cleared in the developed world to make way for new roads and housing developments. Rainforests are disappearing because of farming, dams, ranching and logging for fuel and mining.

■ **Effect:** We need trees to take in harmful carbon dioxide and release oxygen, which we need to breathe. Burning trees adds to the amount of carbon dioxide in the air, which adds to global warming. Since 1960, fifty per cent of the rainforests of South America have disappeared and rainforests cover less than six per cent of the earth's surface. Deforestation also leads to soil erosion.

■ **Solution:** Partake in tree-planting schemes and choosing products that have an FSC mark. The FSC mark means that the timber product you are buying comes from a forest that has been well managed or sustainably managed. Last year Ireland imported €145 million worth of tropical hardwood trees like mahogany and rosewood.

Nuclear Pollution

■ **Cause:** Another way of creating electricity is by **nuclear power**, which creates **radioactive waste**.

Sellafield Nuclear Reprocessing plant

■ **Effect:** Radioactive waste remains a threat to the environment for up to 10,000 years. The effects of accidents at nuclear plants like the one in Chernobyl in Belarus is well known to Irish people through the work of Adi Roche and the Chernobyl Children's Fund. Ireland does not have any nuclear power plants but the Sellafield nuclear plant, off the coast of Cumbria in England, is a threat. A campaign was run by Ali Hewson in 2002 to try and put pressure on the British government to close Sellafield. Irish people calling for the closure of the plant sent 1.3 million postcards.

Tony, Look me in the eye and tell me I'm safe.

This postcard is part of a campaign targeting:

- Tony Blair
- Prince Charles
- Norman Askew

(the head of British Nuclear Fuels)

asking them to shut down Sellafield.

Tear this postcard off and post it on or by the 19th April 2002.

Greetings from Ireland

■ **Solution:** Use renewable energy sources like **wind**, **solar** and **wave power** to create electricity. We should have more controls on safety in nuclear power plants and a global ban on the testing of nuclear weapons.

Danger for Wildlife

■ **Cause:** Different species of wildlife are disappearing because of the destruction of forests, the trade in exotic animals and luxury goods like fur coats and ivory.

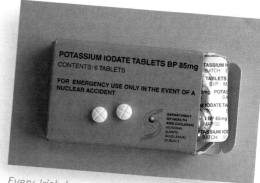

Every Irish household received iodine tablets to be used in the event of a nuclear disaster

■ **Effect:** Many species of animals are becoming extinct.
Less research is possible into new drugs from plants because of disappearing forests.

■ **Solution:** We should have more game reserves and wildlife parks, as well as more controls on the destruction of forests and farmland.

Activities

1. What is green energy?
2. What is global warming?
3. What is the Kyoto Agreement?
4. Why is the ozone layer important?
5. What damage is caused by acid rain?
6. What is the effect of the rainforests being cut down?
7. Why are certain species of animals in danger of extinction?

Study ⑪ So What Can You Do?

In the following articles you can find out how students went about taking action on their local environment.

Keep It Green

Green Schools is a Europe-wide environmental programme that encourages schools to make lifestyle changes that protect and improve the environment.

Pupils from Ringsend Technical Institute have been working very hard since the beginning of the school year to ensure that their school is awarded a European Green Flag – an award given to schools around Europe that successfully implement the programme.

The Green Schools Committee, which was set up to run the programme, is made up of pupils from all levels in the school.

The first thing the committee did was a survey of all of the bins in the school to find out the volume and type of waste currently being produced by the school. These are the results:

- *Paper 54%*
- *Plastic 17.5%*
- *Cans/Tins 5.5%*
- *Bottles 13.3%*
- *Organic 10.6%*
- *Other 2.5%*

The biggest problem in our school is the amount of waste paper we send to landfill every week. Our target is to minimise this as much as possible and to recycle a massive fifty per cent of our waste. This will be achieved by reusing as much of our waste paper as possible for rough work in the classroom. We will also give waste paper to the local crèche for use in their art classes.

We will put specially made paper bins throughout the school and these bins will be emptied daily into our green wheelie bins provided by Dublin City Council. Through our

Find out how many aluminium cans your school could recycle every week

Green Schools Programme we hope to be able to recycle nearly all our paper.

Since we know what the problem is and have devised a method of solving it, the main focus of our Green Schools Programme will be on ensuring that everybody in the school (including teachers and our principal) put paper in the right bins.

Once our programme is established we hope to expand it to include plastics, tins/cans and organic waste.

Minimisation and recycling of waste is a very important lesson that everyone must be prepared to learn. Pupils of Ringsend Technical Institute

*are leading the way – and are an example for the rest of the community!
(News Four)*

*(Green Schools is run in Ireland by An Taisce in partnership with local authorities throughout
the country.)*

Secondary Schools Win Anti-litter Awards

*Galway Mayor Councillor Donal Lyons presented fifty prizes in City Hall on
Wednesday 1 May to students from secondary schools who took part in
the anti-litter poster and slogan awareness competition organised by the
Environment Section of Galway City Council.*

*Presenting the prizes, Mayor Lyons
complimented the secondary school students and
their schools on the quality and quantity of work
entered, saying he was particularly pleased to see
that 572 students from seven out of ten city schools
took part in the competition. 'Litter is not just
unsightly, it can damage our tourist industry and
reputation. Cleaning up litter costs the city in excess
of €700,000 yearly, money that would be much better spent on
community services.'*

*Congratulating the winners the mayor said, 'Our prize fund
of €5,000 shows Galway City Council is serious about
enlisting the secondary schools and students in the anti-litter
awareness campaign. What's important in this type of
competition is not the individual winners, but the numbers
who get involved.' A selection of winning posters was on display at
the prize-giving ceremony.*

*In the 'slogan' segment of the competition, slogans varied from short
'Bin there, dumped that', and sweet **'Pollution thrives where litter lies'** to
grim reality **'Keep Galway neat cause we don't want it to smell like feet'**!*

(Galway City Council website.)

National Spring Clean

The National Spring Clean campaign is another way that people take action on the environment
in their community. The National Spring Clean campaign is Ireland's biggest **anti-litter**

campaign and encourages groups from all walks of life to take pride in their environment. National Spring Clean encourages people to take action against litter.

The Young Environmentalist Awards

The Young Environmentalist Awards scheme is for all second-level schools and youth groups, organised by Ballygowan/ECO. Projects can be done on one of five main environmental areas – air, water, energy, waste or biodiversity.

The following is a summary of a project that won an award in the Junior section.

What can I do?

Anyone can get involved in National Spring Clean:
• Schools • Local Authorities • Youth Groups
• Businesses • Voluntary Groups • Individuals
Just choose an area nearby to clean up, and get together with family, friends or colleagues to make your event fun.

How do I get involved?

You can either return the registration form inside this leaflet or ring the Hotline number – 01 4544794, or register on-line at: www.antaisce.org/projects/nsc.html A FREE Clean-Up Kit is provided to all volunteers who register through An Taisce. The Clean-Up Kit includes useful information on the following:

• How to organise an event • Posters • A ready-made press release • How to continue your environmental improvements • Protective tabards for your group to wear during the clean-up • Information on waste reduction, reuse and recycling • Refuse sacks

CSPE and Green Schools

For Junior Cycle classes, National Spring Clean can be organised as an Environmental Action project for Civic, Social and Political Education. Many Green-Schools have held Spring Cleans for their 'Day of Action' to inform the wider community about litter and waste issues.

Below: Minister Noel Dempsey, Patricia Oliver, An Taisce, Dermot Hopkins, Coca-Cola, Minister Dan Wallace and Today FM's favourite DJ Ian Dempsey pictured with two litter ladies at the launch of last years National Spring Clean

Nicola and Tracy from St Paul's Secondary School, Greenhills chose energy as the theme for their Young Environmentalist project, as they were concerned at how much energy was being wasted in school and at home and wanted to put a stop to it. They actively campaigned to reduce the amount of energy wasted in their school by placing signs around every light switch in the school with a sharp message, 'When can a light get a break around here!! You turned me on, now turn me off.'

An energy-saving newsletter was distributed and displayed in their local library and the girls made their energy-saving ideas available to as many people as possible by designing and launching their very own energy-saving website – www.energywise.freeservers.com.

Winners of Ballygowan/ECO awards

Environmentally Friendly Products

Another way that you can be a good steward of the planet is by buying environmentally friendly products. Think about the following the next time you are buying something.

- Consider the type of packaging used. Is the product wrapped in plastic, polystyrene or paper? Look for products that are wrapped in biodegradable packaging.
- Does the product have a short life cycle or is it disposable? For example, battery-operated products, disposable nappies and disposable razors have a short life span. Look for products that last.

Study ⑫ Action Project Ideas

New School/Rules

1. You and your classmates could put together a leaflet or booklet for next year's first years. The leaflet could include information on clubs and after-school activities, what to do if they are aware of a bullying incident and other information that would help them to make school a success.

2. Carry out a survey on bullying (example on p. 209). You could use your results as part of an awareness week or a leaflet on bullying and how to deal with it.

Rights and Responsibilities

1. Contact a voluntary organisation and design an information poster about their work. This could be displayed around the school.

2. Many national organisations like the **Irish Red Cross** have local branches. Invite a local member of one of these organisations into your school to talk about their work.

3. Run a poster campaign or awareness week in your school highlighting human rights abuses in national and international situations.

4. Organise a fundraising event (e.g. cake sale) for an organisation whose work you are interested in.

5. Invite a member of a senior class who is involved in an **Amnesty International** club or **St Vincent de Paul** group to give a talk to your class on what they do.

stewardship

6. Carry out a survey to find out how wheelchair friendly your school is.

Environment

1. Start a school clean-up campaign and an anti-litter campaign.

2. Run a recycling campaign, placing paper and can bins around the school.

3. Invite a guest speaker from a local or school environmental club into your class to explain the club's work.

4. Organise the planting of flowers or shrubs around the grounds of your school.

5. Design a poster or information leaflet on animal care.

6. Invite a guest speaker from the ISPCA to talk about endangered species or animal care.

7. Run an awareness week on environmental issues.

Remember to look back over the action ideas that are suggested throughout the chapter for more topics for an action project.

In chapter 5 you will find advice and helpful hints on how to do posters, leaflets, surveys, interviews, petitions and fundraising events.

In the assessment section of chapter 5 you will find a breakdown of exactly what kind of information is needed for all sections of a Report on an Action Project (RAP) and a Coursework Assessment Book (CWAB).

Study 13 Revision Questions

(Revised Exam Format – 80 Marks)

Section 1 – 18 Marks
Answer ALL questions.

1. (a) Which **two** of the following politicians were involved in the Northern Ireland peace process?

    Put a tick in the box opposite the correct names. (4 marks)
    - (i)   George Mitchell   ❐
    - (ii) Mo Mowlam   ❐
    - (iii) Mary O'Rourke   ❐
    - (iv) Proinsuas de Rossa   ❐

   (b) Indicate whether the following statements are **True** or **False** by placing a tick beside the correct answer. (4 marks)

		True	False
(a)	Bullying always involves physical violence.	❐	❐
(b)	Amnesty International does not oppose the death penalty.	❐	❐
(c)	Children have the right to play.	❐	❐
(d)	A compromise is when two sides meet each other halfway to solve a conflict.	❐	❐

2. Fill in the missing words in the following sentences. (4 marks)
   - (a) To say that all football fans are hooligans is called _____.
   - (b) _____ won the Nobel Peace Prize for his efforts to bring about equality between all South Africans.
   - (c) The organisation known as _____ _____ concerns itself with the needs and rights of the homeless.
   - (d) Cutting down rainforests contributes to the _____ effect.

rights and responsibilities

3. In the boxes provided below match the letters in row X with the corresponding numbers in row Y. The first pair is completed for you.   (6 marks)

X	A	B	C	D	E	F	G
Y	7						

X

A. Pavee Point is
B. The United Nations Declaration is
C. The family is
D. The Kyoto Agreement is
E. Rights and responsibilities
F. Voice is
G. Coal, gas and oil

Y

1. an organisation that concerns itself with the environment.
2. the most common unit in society.
3. are non-renewable sources of energy.
4. an international treaty to fight global warming.
5. go hand in hand.
6. a charter of rights every human is entitled to.
7. an organisation that concerns itself with Travellers.

Section 2
Answer ALL questions numbered 1, 2 and 3 below.
Each question carries 14 marks.

1. Look at the pictures below and answer the questions that follow.

(a) Name a human right you think the people in each of these pictures are being denied. (2)

(b) Name **one** document drafted by the United Nations for the protection of human rights. (2)

(c) Name **two** countries that you know of where human rights are being denied. (4)

(d) Name **two** organisations that concern themselves with the protection of human rights. Describe two actions that one of these organisations has taken to protect human rights.

First organisation (1)

Second organisation (1)

First action (2)

Second action (2)

2. Examine the photograph and answer the questions that follow.

(a) What are these people protesting about? (2)

(b) Name **two** other groups in society that may have their rights denied and say which right they are being denied.

Groups (2)

Rights (4)

(c) Explain what you understand discrimination to mean. (2)

(d) Describe **two** actions you would take in your school to highlight the issue of the denial of human rights for a particular situation.

Action 1   (2)

Action 2   (2)

3. Read the text below and answer the questions that follow.

'Our ancestors taught us to share what we gather in a day. We must keep the forest as the home of animals but also for pure water and air. The only reason it still exists is that we have taken care that it's not destroyed. We need the trees for thatch, for medicines and because they provide fruit. The forest is our home.'

Shipibo Indians, Peru

(a) What did the ancestors of the Shipibo Indians teach them?   (2)

(b) List **two** reasons why the forest is so important to the Shipibo Indians.   (2)

(c) Name **one** of the biggest rainforest regions in the world.   (2)

(d) Name **one** environmental issue that concerns you, say **why** you are concerned about it and state **two** actions that you could take over the issue.

The issue   (2)

Why you are concerned   (2)

Action 1   (2)

Action 2   (2)

Section 3
Answer ONE of the questions numbered 1, 2 and 3 below.
Each question carries 20 marks.

1. Amnesty International's main weapons are letter writing and lobbying.

(a) Describe how you would organise a campaign in your school to highlight the work of Amnesty International.

(b) Describe in words or draw an outline of a poster which would highlight a right contained in the UN Convention on the Rights of the Child.

2. *'I object to violence because when it appears to do good, the good is only temporary – the evil it does is permanent.'*

Mahatma Gandhi

(a) Write an article for your school magazine on solving conflict situations peacefully. In your article use examples from recent history of well-known people who have successfully done this.

(b) Make up a slogan that would help students understand the importance of **compromise**.

(c) What was the major issue that led to the suspension of the Northern Ireland Assembly in 2002?

3. Imagine you have invited a member of a local environmental group to talk to your CSPE class.
   (a) Describe how you would organise and prepare for the visit.
   (b) Outline the type of issues you would discuss with your visitor.
   (c) Describe how you would organise a campaign to keep your school a litter-free zone.

 Now test yourself at **www.my-etest.com**

stewardship

02 chapter

SECTION A – YOUR COMMUNITY ■ **SECTION B** – COMMUNITIES IN ACTION

In chapter 1 you saw how you are a member of and participate in your family community and your school community. You saw how being a member of these communities brings with it certain rights and responsibilities, and how you as an individual can affect those communities by your actions. Schools and families are part of the local community. We are all involved in our local community because we interact with it all the time.

Study 14 What is a Community?

We belong to many **communities** at the same time.

- The family community is the first and most important community that we are members of. Other members of our family could be parents, guardians, brothers, sisters, grandparents, aunts and uncles.

- The school community is usually the next group that we join and this group is made up of other students as well as school staff such as teachers, secretaries and caretakers.

- The neighbourhood community is made up of families who live near each other and who often meet each other.

- The local community is made up of many of these neighbourhoods together, like in a housing estate, village or town.

Each larger community is made up of many smaller communities and we all participate in these communities at different levels.

How much do you know about your **local community** and how much do you take part in it? The following questions can help you to gather information about your community. Either answer them yourself or use the questions to interview a classmate about his or her community.

Activities

1. How large is your community?

2. Who would you consider to be the most important members of your community and why?

3. Have there been any famous people from your community?

4. Which important historical events took place in your area?

5. Which historical buildings or landmarks are in your area?

6. Which festivals take place in your area?

7. Name an area in your locality that you find interesting and say why.

8. Is there anything that you would consider an eyesore in your area? If so, explain why.

9. Where in your area do people go to meet each other?

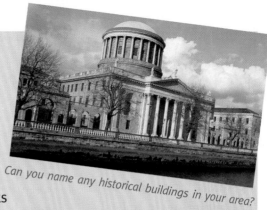

Can you name any historical buildings in your area?

What festivals take place in your area?

ACTION

Research: Communities evolve and change over time. Find out how your community has changed in the past fifty years by interviewing an older member of your community.

Study 15 Local Government

Every local community is made up of various amenities and services that members from the locality use on a daily basis. Here are some of the facilities that might be in your locality:

- post office
- fire station
- public park
- sports club
- swimming pool
- car park
- garda station
- library.

Local Authorities

Many of the services and amenities that we use every day, like getting water from the tap or visiting the park, are the responsibilities of the local authority. **There are four different kinds of local authorities in Ireland:**

Local Authority Areas

- twenty-nine county councils, e.g. Fingal
- five city councils, e.g. Cork
- five borough councils, e.g. Kilkenny
- seventy-nine town councils, e.g. Killarney

There are 114 local authorities in Ireland. Local authorities are part of the local government system. The Department of the Environment and Local Government is responsible for the local authorities.

Why Do We Need Local Authorities?

The national government that sits in the Dáil is not as familiar with the needs of an area as the people living there are, so this two-tier system of government, i.e. local government and national government, gives people a chance to make their voices heard and to influence change for the benefit of their community.

What Do they Do?

Some of the main areas or **programme groups** that local authorities have responsibility for are:

- housing and building
- road transportation and safety
- water supply and sewage
- environmental protection, including rivers, lakes, air and noise
- recreation and amenities
- planning.

rights and responsibilities

Who Runs Local Government?

Local councillors and **city** and **county managers** run local government. They in turn report to the Minister for the Environment and Local Government. Local councillors are elected by the people of an area every five years. Many local councillors are members of political parties and use their experience of local government as a stepping-stone for election to national government, i.e. to become TDs.

Cork County Council – the Strategic Policy Committee for South Cork, chaired by Cllr Barry Cogan, with Tom Stritch (right), Director of Service Southern Division, and Cllr Tomas Tyan, Vice-Chairman Southern Division

Anyone over eighteen years of age can run for office. The job is voluntary: there is no salary. However, an annual allowance is given to cover such expenses as travel, telephone and postal charges. Most local authorities hold meetings every month. At these meetings important decisions are made on how much will be spent in an area and on what. Decisions made by the councillors are reached by **voting**.

As local councillors' jobs are part-time, city and county managers are employed on a full-time basis to carry out the decisions made by the councillors.

Who Pays for Local Government?

Running local government costs money. It is paid for by:

- grants from the national government
- grants from the European Union
- money raised in the locality from such things as parking meters and charges from local swimming pools and libraries
- money raised from motor tax
- borrowing.

What is a Development Plan?

Each local authority is responsible for drawing up a **development plan** for its area. This is usually done every five years. A development plan covers such topics as:

- the development of run-down areas
- the development and improvement of parks and public areas
- road improvements
- preservation of historical buildings
- what sort of land should be used for housing, schools, factories and shops. This is called **zoning of land**.

Have you ever seen the development plan for your area?

Following approval by the councillors the draft development plan is put on public display for at least three months in places such as libraries. Any person can make an objection to the plan if they wish.

Every building requires **planning permission**. If any individual or group disagrees with a decision made by a local authority to either grant or refuse planning permission, they can go to **An Bord Pleanála***. An Bord Pleanála will look at the case again.

Everyone has the right to a say in the future planning and development of their area.

> * An Bord Pleanála is a body set up by the government to deal with planning applications that cause difficulty or controversy.

Activities

1. Which facilities do you use in your area?
2. What facilities do you consider to be the most important and why?
3. What services and amenities would be available in your ideal community?
4. Draw a map of your ideal area. Remember to include essential services like hospitals and schools as well as recreational facilities.
5. Who is in charge of local government?
6. Using the map on p. 54, name the different kinds of local authorities in your county.

democracy

7. Which **programme groups** (see p. 54) do you think are responsible for the following services?
   ● providing accommodation for Travellers
   ● providing street lights
   ● providing a sewage system
   ● getting rid of waste
   ● running libraries and swimming pools
   ● looking after parks
   ● street cleaning and litter prevention.

8. How often are local councillors elected?
9. How do local authorities make decisions?
10. Who carries out the decisions of a local authority?
11. In your opinion, why would a person wish to become a local councillor?
12. Name a local councillor from your area.
13. What does a development plan cover?
14. What does zoning of land mean?
15. How can you influence your area's development plan?
16. Why would a person go to An Bord Pleanála?
17. Why do you think development plans are necessary?

ACTION

Research: Using your local newspaper, find out which issues have caused difficulties at council meetings recently and present your findings in class.

Study 16 Interview with a Councillor

The following interview with John Ryan, a Labour councillor, explains the kind of work he is involved in and some of the reasons why people become involved in local politics.

Why did you become a counciller?

I went for election to Limerick City Council as a result of being actively involved in a number of local issues and not agreeing with the way the sitting councillors were

dealing with these issues. For example, the city dump was a disgrace and little was being done to change it. A young cyclist was knocked down and killed on our road but the city council would not install speed ramps. There were no proper playgrounds in the city, and some areas of the city with major social problems were being ignored.

Councillor John Ryan

Why did you become a councillor?

Local councillors decide on the yearly budget for the city council and can direct spending towards certain issues and areas. A councillor is involved in the development plan for their area, which must be agreed by the council and includes what land can be used for (zoning), how the city is to be developed and what the priorities are for the next five years. Councillors bring forward to the city council the needs of their constituents by raising these issues at council meetings.

From 2004 elections will be counted electronically

Why is it important to vote?

Because if you don't you have no input into who gets elected and who makes the decisions about your neighbourhood. By not voting, and particularly young voters not voting, you are saying you don't want to change those in power. If you are happy to let others decide who is best to represent your opinions then don't vote. But don't give out about what politicians do if you don't vote, because you didn't want a say in who should be elected.

It is important for young people to be involved in politics?

Yes. It is vitally important, not because young people know what to do or have all the answers, but because older people don't always know what to do (even though they think they do) and don't have all the answers (even though they think they do). Society is made up of various groups, many of whom are not listened to or represented on local councils. Young people are one such group but nobody is going to come along and offer them places. You have to fight to be heard and elected.

development

 **Activities**

1. How did John Ryan become interested in local politics?
2. Name two things local councillors do for their area.
3. Give one reason why a person should vote in their local elections.
4. According to John, why should young people get involved in politics?
5. What issues in your neighbourhood concern you and what action would you like to see taken on these issues?

Children's Councils

In Strasbourg, France a mayor wanted children's advice on a plan for the town so he got the schools to elect a children's council. Now, in over 700 towns and villages across France, children elect their own official council to shadow the work of the adult council and approve their decisions. They also choose '**action programmes**' to carry out some of the ideas they have promoted. This movement has had an impact right up to national level. Politicians see it as a way of giving young people experience of politics and getting them interested in their local communities. The idea has spread to other countries like Italy, Austria and Germany.

Would you like to be a member of a student's council?

 **Activities**

1. What do you think of children's councils? Give reasons for your answer.
2. If you were on a children's council for your area, what ideas would you bring up and how would you get your ideas carried out?
3. Write a letter to your local authority telling them about children's councils in other countries and asking them how young people in Ireland can get their ideas heard by local government.

Research: Interview a local councillor and find out why that person became a councillor and how he/she tries to help improve the locality. The councillor could be invited to speak to your class.

Study 17 The Wasteland

Development in a Community

The process of **development** in any community may be controversial, because what one person sees as being good for their community, another may see as being bad. Planning issues are sometimes the cause of conflict in a local community. Different groups within a community may have different views about how a piece of wasteland, for example, might be developed.

There are many people who live and work in the locality who are interested in what happens to it, because it is a valuable site in the middle of an urban area.

This piece of wasteland is about to be put up for sale for redevelopment

Read what the various interest groups in the community want to do with the land and answer the questions that follow.

'We, the members of the community association, think that the site should be used as a **community centre**. It could provide a focus point for the community, a drop-in centre for the unemployed, social evenings for the elderly and a place for young people to meet. We have been fundraising for a number of years, and with the help of a government grant we could afford to buy the site and erect the community centre. We think that a community centre would be the best way to get the young people off the streets and reduce crime and vandalism in the area.'

Mr Lawless – chairperson of the local community association

'I want to build a **cinema**, a small **shopping complex** and a **nightclub** on the site. I already have tenants for the shops and the nightclub if I can buy the site. This would bring a larger range of amenities to the area, which I believe would help tourism, especially the local hotel and B&Bs, as well as creating employment.'

Mr Brown – local property developer

'We think that the area should be turned into a **park**. We believe that the town needs more trees and open green spaces, not car parks creating more pollution.'

Ms Nolan – member of the local environmental group

'The proposal to put a nightclub on the site is totally unacceptable to the local residents. We would be kept up all night with the noise of people shouting on their way home, revving cars and beeping horns. If the local authority gives permission for Mr Brown's proposed development, the residents' association will appeal the decision to An Bord Pleanála.'

Mr Ryan – local resident

2

'I want to do what is best for the community. I think that Mr Brown's proposal is the best because it would bring business to the area. I feel that the environmentalists don't appreciate the benefits of this.'

Ms Kerins – local politician

Activities

1. There are three proposals for the development of this site. Choose one and suggest more reasons why that proposal should go ahead.

2. Which proposal do you think would benefit the community the most? Give reasons for your answer.

3. In groups of three, choose one interest group and prepare a role-play (three to five minutes) that you would argue at a public meeting. Make sure that each interest group is represented. Two students and the teacher could chair the meeting and decide which interest group makes the strongest case.

4. Imagine you are a newspaper reporter. Write an article briefly describing the main arguments of each interest group and how the meeting ended.

5. Develop a list of arguments for and against the following facilities in your area:
   ● youth club
   ● Travellers' halting site
   ● incinerator
   ● amusement arcade
   ● landfill site (dump).

ACTION

Discussion/Essay: Community development should only be left to elected councillors and community leaders.

Study 18 A Local Environmental Officer

Local authorities now employ environmental officers who work with the local community and try to bring about change on environmental issues locally. Read the following interview with Sadhbh O'Neill, environmental officer for Kilkenny County Council.

What does your job as environmental officer for the county council involve?
I work with schools and local communities to promote waste reduction, composting and recycling. I organise competitions, events and demonstrations to show people what recycling facilities are available in their local area. Sometimes I organise week-long promotions such as Real

Sadhbh O'Neill (back, fifth from left), Environmental Officer with members of a local community in Kilkenny

Nappy Week where we highlight the environmental benefits of using washable nappies. I also organise composting demonstrations to show people how to compost their waste and sell composters to the public. I am responsible for locating all the new recycling facilities. Kilkenny County Council now has facilities for recycling glass, cans, food cans, newspapers, magazines and plastic PET bottles at over forty recycling centres (though not all facilities are available at each location).

What aspects of your job do you particularly enjoy?

My job is great because the public are so supportive of our work. It is easier to convince people to recycle and compost when we actually offer them help, advice, information and facilities. Also, I love visiting schools because young children even as young as four or five are an inspiration. One school in Kilkenny with a Green Flag now produces no waste at all and they grow their own vegetables in the school garden. If everyone could match the enthusiasm of young people we could solve all our environmental problems.

Why do you think there is a need for an environmental officer attached to the council?

The county council has so many duties to perform that sometimes public awareness can be left out. In the case of waste management, the public needs advice and information if they are to help the council implement its policies. Also, there is no point putting facilities like bottle banks in place and then not telling anyone about them! In my role I help the public understand what the council is trying to achieve and it encourages the public to work with us to solve problems.

How does the local community help you in your work?

In some ways the real leaders are local communities and voluntary organisations. Local authorities are responsible for policy but it is up to individuals and communities to make the necessary changes towards a sustainable community. So very often the ideas and the on-the-ground work come from community organisations. We just supply the information and resources needed. In some communities there is an effort now to move towards making their town an eco-village by making it litter-free and meeting the highest environmental standards.

How did you become interested in environmental issues, and did you need any special training for this job?

I worked for many years as a campaigner with environmental organisations, including Earthwatch and An Taisce. This work gave me a particular insight into waste problems *but also the global dimension to many environmental issues. Before that I was actually a politician for a few years while a student in Trinity College. I was a member of Dublin Corporation from 1991–95 representing the Green Party, and this experience too showed me the inner workings of local authorities. I saw environmental problems as very political problems requiring political debate and attention. At that time there was very little recycling because dumping into landfill was so cheap. Thankfully that has changed now and recycling is becoming widespread and economically competitive.*

Activities

1. Name four things that Sadhbh O'Neill does as part of her job.
2. What did the school mentioned in the interview do to get a Green Flag?
3. What does Sadhbh say is the job of the local authority?
4. Who does she believe are the people who can bring about most change?
5. How did Sadhbh become involved in environmental issues?
6. What environmental changes would you like to see in your area?

Different people come together in communities over issues that concern them and affect their lives. Groups are often formed representing the different viewpoints of the people from within the community, and they attempt to bring about change on an issue that concerns them.

Study 19

Case Studies - Communities Taking Action

Read **one** or more of the following case studies about communities taking action and answer the questions that follow.

Case Study 1 – A Community in Action

The residents of a town in County Laois were concerned about the lack of services the county council were providing in their town. Read how they went about taking action.

Durrow protests over Laois Council 'neglect'

The people of Durrow in Co. Laois have taken to the streets to protest at what they claim is a lack of interest by Laois County Council in their town.

Members of the local community council say they are tired of writing letters to the county council complaining about potholes, poor lighting and other inadequate services in the town and getting no response.

'We were at the end of our tether. I simply refused to write any more letters to the county council. They were just filed away and I felt it was a waste of time and money in the end,' said Ms Anne Vaugh, secretary of the community council . . .

Footpaths in Durrow were so uneven they were a liability and even new lighting installed in one area was so poor 'you couldn't see your hand'.

She said it was so dark in the town square people were afraid to use the public phone box at night. 'Down the road in Abbeyleix you would be absolutely blinded by the lights,' she said.

The town also needed traffic-calming measures to slow through traffic.

rights and responsibilities

There were calming measures in nearby Abbeyleix and Cullohill but again none in Durrow. 'The speed of traffic is just ridiculous. It's a miracle that nobody has been knocked down.'

She pledged the community council would be a thorn in the council's side until some progress was made.

She added that locals hadn't ruled out blocking traffic on the main Dublin/Cork road on a busy Friday evening to draw attention to their plight.

She said, however, that the council had been busy filling potholes in the town just before this week's protest, which attracted over 150 people . . .

'We have no council worker, nobody sweeping the streets and no services whatsoever. We pay car tax and income tax but there is nothing coming back to Durrow.'

In a statement, the county council rejected some of the assertions made by local people. It said traffic route lighting and public lighting in Durrow was 'of a comparable standard' with other towns and villages in the county.

'Regarding the footpaths in Durrow, we acknowledge that there are sections in need of repair but we are looking at a programme of improvements which will be considered at the roads area meetings due to be held next week.'

(*Eithne Donnellan*, The Irish Times)

 Activities

Case Study 1

1. What two actions have the people of Durrow taken to draw attention to their concerns?
2. Name four things the people from Durrow are concerned about.
3. What other form of protest is being considered by the people of Durrow?
4. Name one way the council pay for the services they provide that is mentioned in the article.
5. In the article, what does the county council say about the concerns raised?

Case Study 2 – A Community in Action

The community of Foxford was concerned about the closure of a bank in the town. Read about how the community took action on this issue.

Groups boycott bank in protest

A community in the west of Ireland is boycotting the Bank of Ireland in protest after it closed its branch in the town.

Residents in Foxford, Co. Mayo are up in arms over the move and they have announced they are closing their accounts.

Twenty-two organisations, representative of the 1,000-strong population, said they were taking the action as a symbolic gesture which they felt would give the financial institution a 'bloody nose'.

The action is being co-ordinated by the Foxford and District Community Council.

At the end of March the bank closed the sub office after thirty years, citing it was no longer financially viable to continue the service.

Community Council vice-chairman Brendan Sherry said in dealing with the issue of closure and in refusing to provide even an ATM in place of the branch, the Bank of Ireland had insulted the whole community.

Mr Sherry felt that in light of Bank of Ireland's decision to proceed with the closure of up to one in five of its branches, it was clear that Foxford and a few other vulnerable communities were used by the bank as the litmus test for public reaction.

'The bank can waffle on all it likes about Internet banking and facilitating us in whatever way it can,' he said, 'this does not help pensioners, tourists and the rest of us that have been left without a service. As a symbolic gesture, the people of Foxford, as represented by the twenty-two community groups, intend to close their accounts with Bank of Ireland . . .

Under the umbrella of the organisation they wanted everyone to know that they believed the bank had not treated them fairly.

The list of groups withdrawing their accounts includes Foxford Social Services, the Mayo/Roscommon Hospice Foundation, Foxford Community Games, Foxford Fianna Fáil Cumann, Foxford St Vincent de Paul, St Michael's Church and Brown Memorial Hall.

The community are now waiting on the bank's reaction to the protest.

(*Tom Gillespie,* Irish Examiner)

Activities

Case Study 2

1. How many different groups from the community are taking action?
2. What form of protest are they taking?
3. Who do the residents believe will be affected by the bank's closure?
4. Who is representing the views of the people of Foxford?

Case Study 3 – The Garda Community in Action

Sometimes groups that have a specific role within a community, like the gardaí, take action over an issue that they think would help the people of an area.

The Garda Community in Action

Garda Martin Gibbons (Junior Liaison Officer) and Garda Derek Dempsey (Community Garda) felt that the issues of juvenile crime, alcohol and drug abuse were of concern not only to the gardaí themselves but to all those working with young people.

Martin and Derek decided to take action over these issues by putting together a programme for young people that involved:

- *Visiting primary and secondary schools using quizzes, cartoon strips and discussion to show students the problems that arise from alcohol and drug abuse.*
- *Taking students on an orienteering trip to see if they have learned from the classroom activities. In order to complete the orienteering course successfully, at certain points along the trail students have to find clues and answer questions on crime, alcohol and drug abuse.*

The gardaí work with young people to help prevent juvenile crime

Martin says, 'Everyone assumes that heroin and ecstasy are the biggest drugs. However, the biggest drugs we have are alcohol and tobacco. If you prevent young people from smoking it is unlikely that they will experiment with cannabis. The same applies to under-age drinking. If young people respect alcohol they will not take the next step towards other drugs.'

Once the orienteering challenge is completed students get to play a game called Jail Break. This is where Derek and Martin play the role of judges, while students take turns playing the role of defendants and jury. You can get 'sent down' for not knowing that having a criminal record lasts for life, or that ecstasy can kill you the first time you try it.

Finally, students are presented with a certificate to show that they have completed the Life Orienteering – A Design for Living Programme.

Garda Martin Gibbons says, 'The programme is educational and fun. Students are introduced to a new sport and at the same time learn about the links between crime and drug abuse. It also gives them the opportunity to see gardaí in a positive light as everyone works as a team.'

The course that these two gardaí designed and put into action won the Guinness Living Dublin Awards as well as the AIB Better Ireland Award. They were also overall winners of the Garda Síochána National Merit Award.

 Activities

Case Study 3
1. Over what issue did Gardaí Gibbons and Dempsey take action?
2. Describe how the programme works.
3. Do you think students would learn a lot from a programme like this? Explain your answer.

Case Study 4 – An International Community in Action

In the **developing world** cities are growing rapidly as people leave their rural communities in search of a better way of life. Their way of making a living has been ruined by persecution, famine or deforestation. This has resulted in the emergence of shanty towns (*faevallas* in South America), which lack even the most basic services like clean water, sewage systems, rubbish collection and electricity.

The following case study shows how the residents of the shanty town in Curitiba in Brazil lived in these conditions until they, together with their mayor, decided to take action.

An international community taking action in Curitiba, Brazil – population 1.5 million

The shanty town in Curitiba was built on the banks of the city's river and didn't have any proper roads; the rubbish was not collected and ended up in huge piles on the river's banks. As a result of this the river and its surroundings were stripped of vegetation and full of raw sewage.

A faevalla, or slum, in South America

As a way of stopping this pollution, the mayor offered transport tokens to adults and books and food to children in exchange for the bags of rubbish being delivered to the local dumps. Soon the whole area was cleaned up and landscaped.

The mayor also built special shopping centres so that the mostly unemployed shanty dwellers could sell their own crafts and produce. In

The University of the Environment, built at Curitiba in Brazil

exchange for their work on these projects the shanty dwellers were given food, rent, education and health care.

An old quarry area was turned into a landscaped cultural centre with a specially built University of the Environment, made from old telegraph poles. All school children and their teachers spend a week here learning how their contribution can create practical benefits for the environment.

All these changes have created a huge sense of pride in the people of Curitiba. The involvement of the people themselves and their commitment to their community provided the key to finding solutions to the huge urban problems that they faced.

 Activities

Case Study 4

1. What is a shanty town?
2. List the different ways the people of this area created change.
3. Do you think the University of the Environment will benefit the area? Explain your answer.

Study 20 Do It Yourself!

GAISCE

As you have seen, there are many ways to get involved in your community. Throughout Ireland many young people have got involved in their communities and have won awards for that participation. Awards that have been given to young people include:

- Gaisce – The President's Award
- Guinness Living Dublin Awards
- AIB Better Ireland Awards
- Environmental Endeavour Awards (discussed in chapter 1, Study 11).

Gaisce – The President's Award

Gaisce is the national challenge award from the President of Ireland to young people between fifteen and twenty-five years of age. The purpose of the award is to encourage young people to set and achieve a demanding challenge for themselves in four different areas:

- community involvement

- personal skills, e.g. learning new computer skills
- physical recreation, e.g. team sports
- adventurous activity, e.g. planning a bicycle trip.

In 1999, a group of students and their teacher from Ballymun Senior Comprehensive absailed down a 150-foot tower block in Ballymun to raise funds for charity. This earned them a silver medal each as well as raising £1,000 (€1,270) for Temple Street Children's Hospital.

There are three different awards: Bronze, Silver and Gold. The challenge is about each person trying to achieve his or her own personal best. Participants are not in competition with each other. The focus is on effort and time commitment. A wide range of schools and clubs operate the award, making it easier for young people to take part.

Read about Sandra Wright and one challenge she took on as part of the An Gaisce Award.

Sandra Wright

Sandra Wright is from Ballinspittle in Co. Cork and is very active in the local community as a youth and Tidy Towns leader. She plays the flute, has taken part in the local musical and keeps fit at the leisure centre where she goes swimming.

Sandra has displayed her caring skills by helping at an orphanage in Romania and by raising £10,000 (€12,700) to buy much-needed supplies. Sandra was named as Kinsale Young Person of The Year.

Sandra receiving her award from the President

Here are some of the ways Sandra helped the orphanage:

Fun runs are often used to raise funds for charities

- 'I held an Easter raffle within the school, and many prizes were sponsored. A total of about £500 (€635) was raised.'
- 'I also held a cake sale for the people of Kinsale. I held a church collection in my local area and raised a total of £550 (€700) towards our journey to Romania. This made people very aware of my venture and the reasons for it and to my ➡

delight many people very generously donated sums of money to the fund – which, of course, were not rejected!'

- ⊕ 'I also got together about £200 (€250) worth of children's clothes, which although they had been worn were still in great condition.'
- ⊕ 'Some medical supplies were also collected.'
- ⊕ 'We left for Romania with a total of about £10,000 (€12,700).'

Guinness Living Dublin Awards

The Guinness Living Dublin Awards recognise people's efforts to make Dublin a better place to live, work and visit. The awards are divided into five categories, one of which is for schools.

Here is an outline of how a group of third-year students won the school section of the Guinness Living Dublin Awards.

Award for Killinarden Park Project

Class 3D of Killinarden Community School, Tallaght won first prize in the Guinness Living Dublin Awards (post-primary section) for their CSPE project 'Action on Killinarden Park'. As their action project the class voted to do a project on their local park and to campaign for improvements.

The class was divided into four groups: a photography group, a survey group, a letter-writing group and an art group.

They started out by surveying local people of all ages to find out what people's main concerns about the park were. They sent letters to their local TDs and councillors expressing their concerns.

Students from Killinarden Community School with their Guinness Living Dublin Award

They also mapped and photographed the park in a class visit last

December. They discovered that most people surveyed were concerned about the amount of attacks on young people in the park. They presented the results of the survey to TD Pat Rabbitte, who visited the class. Pat Rabbitte subsequently tabled a question for South Dublin County Council about improving security in the park. There have been significant improvements made to the park of late.

The local community group Killinarden Services Network heard about Class 3D's project. Four members of the class – Edel Redmond, Rachel Blemings, Jenny Disney and Elaine McGrath – were invited down with their teacher, Ms Linda Neary, to a meeting at the Family Resource Centre to present the main points of their project.

Linda Neary submitted the project on their behalf to the Guinness Living Dublin Awards co-sponsored by Dublin Corporation and Dublin Chamber of Commerce. Eight students and their teacher were invited to the Mansion House on 13 October and presented with a framed certificate, a trophy and a cheque for £1,500 (€1,900) to the delight of the class. The class have been interviewed by journalists in the *Irish Independent* and *The Echo* and were also on the local radio station, TCR 107.2 FM. It's great to see young people making a difference!

(Linda Neary, Killinarden Community School, Dublin)

Research: Find out if Gaisce is operated in your school. If so, invite a speaker from a senior class to tell you about the different challenges that have been undertaken by students in the school.

Discussion/Essay: There are no opportunities for young people to get involved in their communities.

Study 21 Ideas for Action Projects

Your Community

1. Find out about the local clubs and organisations that young people in your community could join and make an information leaflet that could be given out in school.

2. Interview an older member of your community and find out how the area has changed.

3. Do a survey of your local community to find out how people think the area could be improved.

4. Find out if there is any action you could take to improve existing amenities, such as the local playground and swimming pool. For example, could they be made more accessible for wheelchair users?

5. Your class could volunteer to help in the Tidy Towns competition or to participate in one of the award schemes outlined in Study 20.

6. Design a poster that could be used to attract tourists to your area.

Local Government

1. Research an issue, such as a planning decision that has caused controversy in your area. You might find local newspapers helpful. You could do a wall display highlighting the issue.

2. Invite a local councillor to give a talk to your class on the work that councillors do.

> Remember to look back over the action ideas that are suggested throughout the chapter for more topics for an action project.
>
> In chapter 5 you will find advice and helpful hints on how to do posters, leaflets, surveys, interviews, petitions and fundraising events.
>
> In the assessment section of chapter 5 you will find a breakdown of exactly what kind of information is needed for all sections of a Report on an Action Project (RAP) and a Coursework Assessment Book (CWAB).

Study 22 Revision Questions
(Revised Exam Format – 80 Marks)

Section 1 – 18 Marks
Answer ALL questions.

1. (a) Which two of the following organisations give awards to Irish people who have worked towards improving their community? (4 marks)

GAISCE

(i)	Guinness Living Dublin Awards	❐
(ii)	Gaisce – The President's Award	❐
(iii)	UNICEF	❐
(iv)	Irish Red Cross	❐

(b) Indicate whether the following statements are **True** or **False** by placing a tick beside the correct answer. (4 marks)

		True	False
(i)	Being a member of a community brings with it certain rights and responsibilities.	❐	❐
(ii)	Gardaí are responsible for providing amenities and services in a locality.	❐	❐
(iii)	One kind of local authority is a county commission.	❐	❐
(iv)	Signing a petition is a form of protest.	❐	❐

2. Fill in the missing words in the following sentences. (4 marks)

(a) The Minister for the _____ and _____ _____ is responsible for local authorities.

(b) One of the main areas or programme groups that local authorities have responsibility for is _____.

(c) Decisions made by councillors are reached by _____.

(d) You must be _____ years of age to run for office in a local election.

3. In the boxes provided below match the letters in row X with the corresponding numbers in row Y. The first pair is completed for you. (6 marks)

X	A	B	C	D	E	F	G
Y	1						

X

A. A local authority is
B. Local councillors
C. The zoning of land is
D. City/county managers
E. An Taisce
F. Local government is
G. An Bord Pleanála

Y

1. responsible for providing accommodation for Travellers.
2. deals with planning applications that cause difficulty.
3. included in an area's local development plan.
4. are elected for a five-year term of office.
5. campaigns for a better environment.
6. the way people influence decisions in their area.
7. carries out decisions made by councillers.

Section 2
Answer ALL questions numbered 1, 2 and 3 below.
Each question carries 14 marks.

1. Examine the headlines below and answer the questions that follow.

Travellers Lobby Council for Halting Site

Local Residents Object to Dump

Methadone clinic opens in residential area

(a) What issues are these newspaper headlines concerned with? (2)

(b) Suggest one form of protest a community could take about an issue that concerns them. (2)

(c) In your opinion, why would a community group contact the media about a local issue that they are concerned with? (2)

(d) Name an issue of local concern that has been in the media recently. (2)

(e) Name a local issue that you are concerned about. State why you are concerned and two actions you could take over the issue.

The issue (1)

Why you are concerned (1)

Action 1 (2)

Action 2 (2)

2. Examine the picture on this page and answer the questions that follow.

(a) What amenities and services do the people in this area have? (2)

(b) State one facility or service you think this community needs. (2)

(c) Give two reasons why you think that the facility or service that you have mentioned above would improve the area. (2)

(d) State how the lack of facilities, e.g. a post office, could affect the lives of the people in a community, and suggest two actions a community could take to try and get this amenity or service for their area.

Facility/amenity (2)

How it affects the community (2)

Action 1 (2)

Action 2 (2)

3. Read the text on the following page and answer the questions that follow.

(a) List two issues that are of concern to this councillor. (2)

(b) Which of the issues mentioned above do you think is important and why? (4)

(c) Name two kinds of local authorities in Ireland. (2)

(d) Suggest three arguments that you would use to try and persuade people to come out and vote in a local election.

Argument 1 (2)

Argument 2 (2)

Argument 3 (2)

Section 3
Answer ONE of the questions numbered 1, 2 and 3 below.
Each question carries 20 marks.

1. Imagine a disused building becomes available and it is proposed it should become a youth club. The local residents are worried it could affect their quality of life.

(a) Describe the arguments in favour of the youth club.

(b) Describe the arguments against the youth club.

(c) Suggest an alternative use for the site and give reasons why.

2. Imagine your local council has proposed to locate a halting site for Travellers in your area. A meeting has been called to discuss the proposal.

(a) Describe the arguments for the proposal.

(b) Describe the arguments against the proposal.

(c) Describe how you would organise such a meeting in order to ensure that all sides are treated fairly and equally.

democracy

GREEN PARTY

Comhaontas Glas

DOMINIC LEONARD

Your Candidate for a Greener New Millennium

I will work with you towards cleaner: { Politics / Environment / Food } for a cleaner future

Environment

Transport

- **LUAS:** no more delays
- **Dublin Bus:** a more efficient, accessible service for all; a shuttle service to the LUAS stops
- **Cycleways:** more of them and designed with the cyclist in mind, not the car
- **Access:** accessible buses, LUAS vehicles, pavements and buildings for people with disabilities
- **Parking:** residents' permits (especially near LUAS stops); proper enforcement of parking laws and disability-only parking

Waste management

- **Recycling:** raising awareness of reusing and recycling, starting at home
- **Littering:** clean up our areas and enforcement of anti-litter legislation

Politics

- Honesty, openness and accountability of local government
- Decentralisation of power and responsibility to local communities

3. Imagine you have invited your community garda to talk to your CSPE class.

  (a) Name and describe two issues of concern that you would like to discuss with him/her.

  (b) Describe what actions you would take in preparation for the visit.

  (c) Suggest an action you could take following the garda's visit to inform others of the work of the community garda.

 Now test yourself at **www.my-etest.com**

03 chapter

SECTION A – OUR STATE ■ SECTION B – THE STATE AND YOU

FIANNA FÁIL
THE REPUBLICAN PARTY

In chapter 2 you learned what a community is and how people participate in their communities. You saw how a local community could take action and bring about change. But individuals or communities can also seek to influence what happens at a national level. The state can be seen as a large grouping of communities. As citizens of Ireland, we should have a basic understanding of the State's political system and structures so that we can exercise power through participation.

Study 23 Democracy and You

The word *democracy* comes from the Greek words *demos*, meaning *people*, and *kratia*, meaning *to rule*. Thus, in a democracy rules and laws are made and agreed by the people of a country, for the people of a country. Laws are passed when a majority of the people agree.

Democracy at work in ancient Greece

The ancient Greeks were the first people to rule this way. Because the voting population was small in ancient Greece (only freemen had the right to vote), all freemen had a chance to have a say directly in how the state was run. This was called **direct democracy**. In Ireland

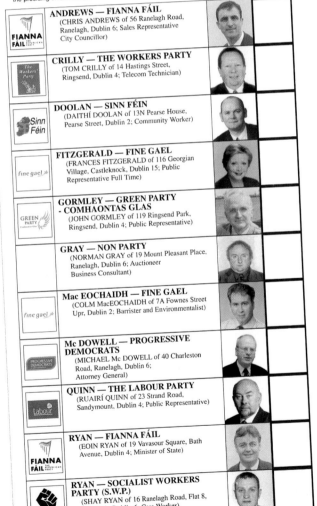

today, with a population of nearly four million people, it would be impossible to run a system where everyone directly has a say. What we do instead is elect people to Dáil Éireann to represent our views, thoughts and ideas on how the country should be run. This is called **representative democracy**. The members of the Dáil represent the different views that people have on running the country.

In Ireland people have the right to vote. Many people believe that citizens have a duty to vote in elections. Some countries (e.g. Belgium) believe that it is such an important duty that a person can be fined for not voting.

In order to vote in an election a person must be eighteen years of age and their name must be on the **Register of Electors**. A person can register at a local post office, garda station or local authority office. If a person is registered to vote,

3

they will receive a polling card in the post a few days before an election. The purpose of polling cards is to allow a person to be identified when they go to vote and to make sure that they only vote once. To try to vote more than once is an offence.

At the **polling station**, which is usually a local primary school, a **ballot paper** is used to record your vote. In our voting system, which is called **proportional representation** or **PR**, a person can vote for as many candidates as appear on the ballot paper. To do this the voter selects their first choice, their second choice, their third choice and so on. Voting is done privately in a **polling booth** so that no one can see a person's choice. This is called a **secret ballot**.

Voting machines were used for the first time in the 2002 general election

A candidate is elected when they reach a **quota**. A quota is the smallest number of votes needed to be elected. Under the PR system people have one vote, but that vote is **transferred** from the voter's first choice to their other choices if the first choice candidate is elected. One of the reasons we have this electoral system is so that a larger section of the people's views can be heard and represented.

There are always more candidates than there are seats in the Dáil. Counting goes on until each candidate is either elected or eliminated. When a candidate reaches the quota it is the job of the **returning officer**, who supervises the counting of the votes, to declare the candidate elected.

In the general election of 2002 electronic voting was introduced on a small scale. **Look at this government information leaflet and see how it works**.

ELECTRONIC VOTING | IT'S EASY

At the next general election you will make history as one of the first voters to vote electronically at an election in Ireland. This leaflet will answer some of the most frequently asked questions in relation to the new voting system.

A Lo-Call service **1890 201 607** is available to answer any further queries you may have.

A more detailed information booklet is also available from your local authority, library, citizen information centre or from the Department of the Environment and Local Government's website at **www.environ.ie**

How will I vote?

It's simple. Follow these four easy steps:-

1. Have your name marked off the register in the normal way and you will be given a token by polling staff
2. Go to the polling clerk at the voting machine and hand over the token
3. Record preferences for the candidates of your choice by pressing the buttons beside the candidates' photographs on the ballot paper displayed on the machine

4. Cast your vote by pressing the "Cast Vote" button

What if I make a mistake?

If you make a mistake or you want to change your mind, simply press the button opposite the candidate's name a second time. This will delete that preference and any other lower preferences and you can then record your new choices.

If I leave the voting machine without pressing the "Cast Vote" button, can I return to press it?

The display on the voting machine will remind you to press the "Cast Vote" button and a notice will be placed near the machine to remind you to do so. Polling station staff may, if the opportunity arises, inform you that you have not pressed the "Cast Vote" button. After these reminders, if you still do not press the "Cast Vote" button, the polling station staff will de-activate the voting machine and you will not be permitted to use it again for that election.

Will I be voting in private?

Yes. The machine will be positioned so that it faces a wall or screen giving the same level of privacy you have under the old system.

Can I get help if I need it?

Polling station staff will be there to help you and to explain how to operate the voting machine.

Can wheelchair users and visually impaired persons use the voting machine?

Wheelchair users can use the voting machine. The Department is investigating the purchase of an attachment for use by visually impaired voters after the initial use of the machine.

What happens if there is a power failure or if the machine breaks down?

The voting machine will operate on a 12 volt battery in the event of a power failure. Votes which have been cast are safe and will not be lost.

The history of malfunction of the voting machine abroad (Holland, and some of the major cities in Germany) is extremely low. However, if a machine does break down, a replacement will be supplied. Where there is more than one machine in a polling station, electors can use the other machines until a replacement arrives.

Electronic voting

rights and responsibilities

There are a number of elections a person in Ireland can vote in.

- A local election – to elect members to the local authority (councils/corporations). Local elections happen every five years.
- A general election – to elect members to national government (the Dáil). A general election must be held every five years.
- A by-election – to elect a new TD if the TD of an area retires or dies.
- A European election – to elect members to the European Parliament. A European election must take place every five years.
- A presidential election – to elect a new president. This happens every seven years. A president can serve two terms of office, but no more than this.

One other way we participate in running the country is by voting in a **referendum**. Our basic laws are written down in a book called the **Constitution**, and if we want to change any of these laws we must hold a referendum. The Constitution can only be changed if a majority of the citizens of Ireland wish so. Our Constitution has been changed a number of times, such as when the people voted to remove the ban on divorce.

Activities

1. Why is our method of governing called representative democracy?
2. Whose views do the members of the Dáil represent?
3. Do you think it is important that a person votes? Give reasons for your answer.
4. What *four* pieces of information does the ballot paper (p. 85) tell you about each candidate?
5. What instruction is written on the ballot paper that tells you how to vote?
6. Make out a ballot paper of your own, modelled on the example given, and then fill it in using the method described above.
7. What is the system of voting in Ireland called?
8. Why do you think voting is done privately in a polling booth?
9. What is a quota?
10. What is a count?
11. What kind of election was last held in the country?
12. What is the Constitution?
13. Besides elections, what else can a person vote in?

Study 24 Your Vote – Use It

A recent report found that some areas in the country had a poor turn-out of people to vote at elections. One of the findings in the report was that many people were unaware of the power of their vote to bring about change for their area. Other findings were that people thought the polling station was too far away or that they believed that their vote would not change anything.

Read the following article to see how different groups in the community came together to encourage people in the area to have their voice heard in government.

Posters of candidates can be seen in every area at election time

Let's Use our Vote

A dynamic campaign has been launched in Ballyfermot to tackle the problem of low voter turn-out in the area.

'Your Power, Your Vote – Use It!' *is the motto of the campaign, a joint initiative between URBAN Ballyfermot, the Vincentian Partnership for Social Justice and the local community. The launch coincides with a telling report by South West Inner City Network (SWICN). This revealed how low voter participation can result in . . . politicians having little incentive to work in those communities.*

It's hoped that the new initiative will encourage people to use their vote to bring about political change. A colourful brochure has been released as part of the campaign, detailing the Active Citizen Programme. This gives information on helping voters decide what issues are important to them, the steps involved in choosing their candidate and general details about the voting process. Sinn Féin representative, Aengus O'Snodaigh, spoke about the importance of the initiative.

'I would welcome this effort to tackle the problem, which seems to affect working-class areas most,' he said. 'They have become disenfranchised and ignored by the politicians. They feel their area has been ignored for so long, all the benefits are going to other areas and they just turn off instead of standing up for themselves and making a point that they are just as valuable as anyone else.'

(Southside People's News)

law

Following this campaign a general election was held and the number of people who came out to vote did increase.

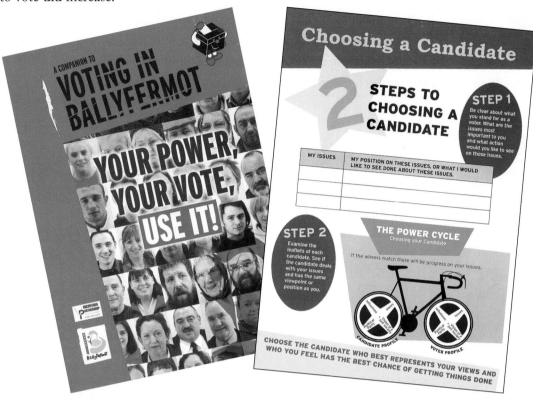

Activities

1. Why did this campaign come about?
2. How can not voting affect an area?
3. What advice on choosing a candidate is given in the brochure?
4. Suggest another slogan that would encourage people to use their vote.

Study 25 Political Parties

A person may vote for a **political party** or an **independent candidate** with whose views they agree. People often vote for a political party in an election. Each political party has a different view on what kind of country we should have. Before an election each political party or independent candidate produces a **manifesto** which states what they will do for the country and its citizens if they are elected.

Bertie Ahern

Fianna Fáil

Fianna Fáil means 'Soldier of Destiny' and is Ireland's largest political party. It was founded in 1926 by Eamon de Valera. It believes in encouraging and developing business. One of its stated aims is 'to secure in peace and agreement the unity of Ireland and its people'. The party has been in government for periods adding up to almost fifty years.

FIANNA FÁIL
THE REPUBLICAN PARTY

Enda Kenny

Fine Gael

Fine Gael means 'Tribes of Ireland' and was formed in 1933. Fine Gael has taken part in many coalition governments in which it has been the majority party. One of the party's stated aims is to create a just society.

fine gael

Pat Rabbitte

The Labour Party

The Labour Party was founded in 1912 by James Connolly, James Larkin and William O'Brien as the political wing of the Irish Trades Union Congress. The Labour Party sees poverty, homelessness and unemployment as the enemies of freedom. Its aim is towards creating a more equal division of wealth and power in society. The Labour Party has taken part in a number of coalition governments.

Labour

Mary Harney

Progressive Democrats

Former Fianna Fáil TDs Des O'Malley and Mary Harney formed the Progressive Democrats in 1985. The party favours tax reform, which it believes would create more jobs. It supports the abolition of the Seanad. The Progressive Democrats party has served in a number of coalition governments.

Progressive Democrats
AN PÁIRTÍ DAONLATHACH

Trevor Sargent

The Green Party

The Green Party was formed in 1981 by Christopher Fettes, an Irish teacher, because of concern about increasing global and local environmental destruction. It believes that as caretakers of the planet we have the responsibility to pass it on in a fit and healthy state. It does not have a leader. Well-known TDs include Trevor Sargent and John Gormley.

GREEN PARTY
Comhaontas Glas

democracy

Sinn Féin

Gerry Adams

Sinn Féin means 'We Ourselves'. It was set up in 1905 by Arthur Griffith. It wants an end to partition, which it sees as the cause of conflict, injustice and division in Ireland. It strives towards a thirty-two-county Ireland, and one of its aims is for a more equal division of wealth and power.

The Socialist Party

Joe Higgins

The Socialist Party was formed in 1996 after a split with the Labour Party. It believes in promoting the rights of workers, the unemployed, women and in social welfare rights.

The terms *right* and *left* politics come from where people sat in the French Assembly after the French revolution (1789). The nobility (conservative), who did not want any change, sat on the right, while those who sat on the left were ordinary people who wanted change.

During a French presidential campaign many people protested against the right-wing candidate, Le Pen

 Activities

1. Choose two of the political parties and state what their aims are.
2. Which political party (or parties) is in government at present?
3. Design a logo for a political party you would like to start, and state three views your party would have on the kind of country we should have.

Interview with a Member of the Green Party

Read the following interview with Trevor Sargent, TD and leader of the Green Party. Find out how and why he became involved in politics.

What made you decide to join the Green Party?

I had an interest in wildlife and conservation at school. When I turned eighteen I wrote to all the political parties seeking their policies. I noticed that none took seriously the global concerns which result in species being made extinct, changing climate resulting in too much dependency on fossil fuels and the widening gap

rights and responsibilities

between the richest and poorest people living on the planet. As a result I became involved in establishing and working for the Green Party.

Trevor Sargent, Green Party

What would a typical week be like for you as a TD?

A typical week would involve meeting people, particularly on Friday evenings and Saturday mornings when I have my constituency clinics. Sundays could also involve attending community events to which I am often invited as a local TD. Monday and Friday I try to spend in the constituency office in Swords or in Balbriggan where I live. Tuesday, Wednesday and Thursday I spend in Leinster House when the Dáil is sitting or committees are meeting. This happens throughout the year except for the month of August. At nighttime also the Dáil can sit until 10.30 pm or later sometimes. Outside of the Dáil, meetings are often called in the evening by residents' groups or sporting organisations, etc. to discuss problems. I could have as many as three meetings on one evening, which involves leaving some meetings early to attend other meetings. From time to time on any day of the week, including Sunday, a radio or TV station can ask for an interview, which may result from a press statement that may be created by a story already in the news.

Why do you think young people should get involved in politics?

I believe that young people are involved in politics, whether they believe it or not, as spending money is a political decision. Buying locally produced products supports local jobs or buying a product that involves using slave labour supports the continuance of slave labour. The biggest way for young people to become formally involved in politics is by, for example, joining a party to ensure that decisions that are taken reflect the interests and needs of young people.

What is the importance of voting in local and national elections?

People who do not use their vote are in fact giving away their power to the people who do vote. The people who do vote are the only ones actually making the decision in the election even though they may be only sixty per cent of the electorate. Although the vote is cast in a secret ballot, councillors sometimes ask at meetings if a person complaining has voted. In a way voting gives one a licence to have one's say after the election as well as on election day.

How can young people influence local and national government?

Young people, like everyone else, can influence local and national government by writing to their councillor or TD, who in turn can table a motion or question based on the views expressed by the writer. Young people can also become more organised and mount campaigns to bring about changes which they believe are necessary. The Green Party is involved with many groups in assisting in the organising of such campaigns.

What are the greatest environmental challenges facing Ireland?

There are many – the biggest one is probably the lack of progress being made to reduce energy demand, which is resulting in growing levels of greenhouse gas emissions. Apart from the effect this is having on climate change, which is causing increased levels of rain and flooding in Ireland, a citizen may well be fined in future as part of Ireland's punishment for not living up to our international obligations under the Kyoto Protocol obligations. Other environmental challenges facing the country are the growing difficulties in meeting the demand for clean drinking water, the loss of habitat for many species of wildlife and the lack of sufficient public transport and cycle routes to give people alternatives to car dependency.

 Activities

1. How did Trevor decide which political party to join?
2. When does he hold constituency meetings?
3. What other work is he involved with outside of the Dáil?
4. Name two ways young people can influence local and national government.
5. What does Trevor say about the effect of growing greenhouse gas emissions in Ireland?
6. If you were joining a political party what issues would be at the top of your agenda?

Research: Find out more information about the youth sections of political parties.

or

Guest Speaker: Invite a member of the youth section of a political party to speak to your class.

law

Ireland is divided into **forty-two constituencies**. In a general election the voters in each constituency elect people to represent them in the Dáil. There are 166 members of the Dáil and they are known as TDs (Teachtaí Dála).

If a single party wins over half of the seats in the Dáil that party can form a **majority government**. If a single party does not get a majority in the Dáil and needs the support of a number of Independents to form a government, this is called a **minority government**. Another type of government that can be formed after a general election is a **coalition government**. This kind of government is made up of a partnership of two or more parties.

The government alone does not govern

Ireland. Among other things, it is guided by the Constitution and the president. Read the following explanations and complete the questions to see how Ireland, the State, is organised.

The Constitution

The Constitution contains the basic laws of our country. It clearly lays out the powers of the president, the government and the three houses of the Oireachtas (the president, Dáil Éireann and Seanad Éireann). It is very important because it acts as a safeguard against the abuse of power and also **protects the rights of citizens**. It guarantees that every citizen has:

- the right to practise religion
- the right to education
- the right to vote
- the right to own and inherit property
- freedom and equal treatment under the law for all citizens.

The President

The head of state is the president of Ireland. The main work of the president is to make sure that any new laws made by the government do not interfere with the rights of the people as written in the Constitution. He/she is the commander and chief of the armed forces. The president also represents Ireland on official visits abroad.

The Dáil

The two Houses of the Oireachtas are called Dáil Éireann and Seanad Éireann. **They decide and make laws**. The Dáil has more power than the Seanad.

President Mary McAleese

The Dáil is made up of **166 TDs** who are elected by the people. During Dáil meetings or sessions they **debate** and **discuss** issues that concern the nation, such as work and unemployment. TDs also question the Taoiseach and ministers about proposed laws and ask them to explain any decisions their department has taken. TDs vote on these new suggestions, or proposals for new laws, as well as on any changes in existing laws. They also vote on how and where money should be spent.

Dáil in session

The Seanad

The Seanad is made up of **sixty senators** who are elected from five panels of people who are experts in different areas affecting the lives of Irish citizens, such

as agriculture, industry and education. They are not directly elected by the people but by members of the incoming Dáil, members of the outgoing Seanad and members of the county councils and corporations. Six members of the Seanad are also elected by the universities and are voted in by graduates. The Taoiseach also nominates eleven candidates.

Seanad in session

democracy

The Seanad can only make suggestions for new laws, but it mainly looks at the changes in the laws which the Dáil wishes to make. Sometimes it suggests changes to that law, but it does not have the power to stop proposals made by the Dáil.

An Taoiseach

The head of the government is called an Taoiseach. He/she is elected by the Dáil following a general election. **The Taoiseach is usually the leader of the political party that has the most members in the Dáil.** The job of the Taoiseach includes appointing ministers to the different government

Bertie Ahern, TD debating in the Dáil

departments, such as Finance and Education. He/she also tries to provide good leadership, runs government meetings and decides when a general election should be held. The Taoiseach also attends meetings with other heads of state of the European Union (EU).

An Tánaiste

The deputy head of the government is called an Tánaiste. He/she acts as head of the government when the Taoiseach is not in the country and may also be responsible for a government department.

The Ministers

The members of the government are called ministers. The number of ministers is set down by the Constitution; it should consist of no less than seven and no more than fifteen ministers. **Ministers are given responsibility for the working of a particular department.** Besides attending government meetings, they must also be ready to answer questions in the Dáil on

Cabinet meeting in session

3

issues concerning their department and take part in important debates about new policies or laws which they have suggested. Ministers also attend meetings of the EU.

Departments

Ministers are in charge of the following government departments:

- Agriculture and Food
- Foreign Affairs
- Arts, Sport and Tourism
- Health and Children
- Defence
- Justice, Equality and Law Reform
- Education and Science
- Communications, Marine and Natural Resources
- Enterprise, Trade and Employment
- Transport
- Social and Family Affairs
- Environment and Local Government
- Community, Rural and Gaeltacht Affairs
- Finance

Department of Foreign Affairs

Government departments have a huge range of responsibilities. For example, the Department of Education is responsible for the civil service, primary schools, post-primary schools, colleges, universities, youth education and adult education. The Department of Justice is responsible for the civil service, laws, courts, prisons and the Garda Síochána.

Civil Service

Civil servants are people who work for the state. **Civil servants advise ministers** about which policies the government should introduce and in what way this might be done. They also carry out the decisions made by the government. Civil servants have a lot of knowledge in a particular area, as they do not change when a new government comes to power. Civil servants are expected to equally serve whatever government is in power and to keep their own political views private.

rights and responsibilities

 Activities

1. Who is the president of Ireland?
2. Can you name some of the important work that the president does?
3. Explain how the Dáil and the Seanad are different.
4. What do TDs and senators do?
5. Name one TD that represents your local area.
6. Who is the Taoiseach?
7. What qualities do you think the head of government should have?
8. Who is the Tánaiste?
9. What is the job of the Tánaiste?
10. Where is the number of government ministers set down?
11. What work does a minister do?
12. How many ministers of government departments can you name?
13. Which departments do you think are the most important and why?
14. Why do government departments need the civil service?
15. Name two kinds of work that the civil service carries out.
16. Why do you think it is important that civil servants keep their political views to themselves?
17. Name the constituency you live in.
18. How many TDs are there in your constituency?
19. Can you name the kind of government that is in power now?
20. Name a member of the Dáil who is an Independent.

ACTION

Quiz: Design a table quiz that could be held in class. The questions could be broken up into three rounds. Below are some examples of the types of rounds and questions you could have.

Round One: How Ireland is Governed
The type of government we have in Ireland is called:
a. democracy **b.** dictatorship **c.** communist

Round Two: The Government

The head of the government in Ireland is called:

a. the president **b.** the prime minister **c.** an Taoiseach

Round Three: Local Government

Local authorities are the responsibility of the Department of:

a. Education and Science **b.** Environment and Local Government **c.** Finance

Information for rounds one and two can be found in this chapter, and information for round three can be found in chapter 2.

Study 28 Dáil na nÓg

Two hundred and fifty children and young people from around the country, aged seven to seventeen years, were invited in 2001 to attend the first Dáil na nÓg. The Minister for Children and the Taoiseach also attended for some of the day to hear the views of the young people who were there.

Dáil na nÓg was set up under the National Children's Strategy. The first goal of the strategy is: **'Children will have a voice in matters which affect them** . . .' so Dáil na nÓg is one way children and young people can have a voice at national level.

Dáil na nÓg meets once a year and a report of the outcomes is published. One thing that is being considered is finding a way for more young people to take part, perhaps by using information technology and setting up local groups.

What Happens?

When the first Dáil na nÓg met in September 2001, part of the day involved workshops, or groups getting together to discuss a certain topic or motion, and then each group voted on the motion. On the day groups discussed four motions:

- education
- environment
- health
- minority groups.

Here is an outline of what happened when the Dáil divided into twenty-one workshops to discuss and think about Motion 1, on education:

That children and young people have a right to express their view in all matters affecting them, taking into account their age and maturity.

That they should be treated with respect in shops and services they use; young people in second level should have a greater say in how their schools are run; children and young people should be listened to more but they should not have too much responsibility; there should be different arrangements for children and young people.

Each workshop or group was made up of fifteen children and was thirty minutes long. The outcomes of the discussions in each group were heard by all the children and young people at a follow-up session after the workshop. The main view that came out from all the discussions that happened in the different groups was that children had the right to **mutual respect** between each other and with adults but too often experienced being excluded in key areas of their lives. Following all the discussions a vote of the membership of the Dáil took place. The breakdown of voting on Motion 1 was as follows:

- 234 votes were cast in support of the motion
- six votes were cast against the motion
- no votes were spoiled.

The Dáil then decided that its support for Motion 1 should be brought to the attention of the Cabinet Committee for Children. The other three motions were discussed and voted on in the same way.

The Rules

Each delegate (person chosen to attend the Dáil) of Dáil na nÓg must follow the rules of the Dáil. They are:

- all delegates agree to arrive and leave on time
- all delegates agree to show respect for all members of the Dáil na nÓg at all times, including:
  - listening and respecting other people's opinions and points of view
  - allowing others the opportunity to speak
  - no shouting or using abusive language or behaviour
- all delegates agree to abide by the directions given by their supervisors and facilitators
- all delegates agree not to leave the venue without first receiving permission from their supervisor.

More information on how to get involved in Dáil na nÓg can be obtained from your Local Development Board.

 **Activities**

1. Why was Dáil na nÓg set up?
2. Would you have voted for or against Motion 1? Give reasons for your answer.
3. Why do you think it is necessary that the young people who attend agree to follow certain rules? Give one reason for each rule.
4. If you were at Dáil na nÓg what would you like to see discussed? Give reasons for choosing the topic or point that you would like to see discussed.

Study 29

A Day in the Life of an Taoiseach

Read the following diary pages to see the kind of work an Taoiseach does in a day.

Wednesday 17 April

(Dáil sitting 2.30 to 10.00 p.m.)

09.00
- Launch book entitled Guide to Elections
  Venue: National Gallery, Clare Street

09.45
- Meeting with an Tánaiste
- Government meeting
- Drop into lunch with Conor Lenihan and members of South Dublin Chamber of Commerce
- Question Time
- Phone call with Scottish First Minister Jack McConnell
- Meeting with Minister of State Martin Cullen
- Briefing on the Order of Business
- Order of Business
- Meeting with Gerry Adams
- Meeting with Minister for Defence and others
- Attend Ireland v USA friendly International Match

democracy

Wednesday 24 April

(Dáil sitting 10.30 a.m. to 8.30 p.m.)

- Meeting at St Lukes
- Photo at Grangegorman with Brendan Goldsmith
- Photocall for Euro 2008 bid
- Briefing on Order of Business
- Order of Business
- Photocall with party leaders for Dublin City Development Board's new website
- Parliamentary party meeting, Leinster House
- Question Time
- 04.00   Photocall for Special Olympics
- Meeting with Parents Committee, St Joseph's School, East Wall. Minister for Education also attending
- Meeting with Síle de Valera
- Officially launch the Killarney Summerfest

Bertie Ahern meeting with President Bush on St Patrick's Day

As well as the entries in his diary, an Taoiseach also undertakes constituency meetings, meets with officials and advisors and takes many phone calls.

(Taken from the diaries of Bertie Ahern, an Taoiseach)

3

🛠 Activities

1. Over these two days, what ministers did the Taoiseach meet with?
2. Why do you think an Taoiseach is asked to do launches and gets his photo taken with different groups?
3. Why do you think a parents committee would want to meet an Taoiseach?
4. What part of an Taoiseach's day do you think was the most interesting and why?

Study 30 An Tánaiste, An Interview

Read the following interview with Mary Harney, TD and find out about the work she does as Tánaiste and leader of a political party.

Mary Harney out canvassing

Why did you get involved in politics?

I got involved in politics full time because a man I respected and admired, Jack Lynch, the then Taoiseach, nominated me to Seanad Éireann.

That was in 1977 when I was twenty-four years old. It was a great honour for me and a progressive move at that time by the Taoiseach to appoint a young woman. In 1982, I was elected to the Dáil in west Dublin.

Jack Lynch believed in peace, democracy and honesty in politics. Politics is about the public interest, how we manage our country best for all our society. There are always important choices to be made in running the country, just as there are choices to be made in every organisation, club and society. The only way to make those choices in a democracy is if people are prepared to stand for election as public representatives.

I've always felt the challenge to do this, on the grounds that if you believe in something, you should get involved. It's for that reason I first started out in politics, and the reason I've stayed with it.

What special responsibilities do you have as leader of a political party?

A political party is a democratic organisation of people who come together on a voluntary basis because they share a belief in how things should be done and what things should be done in the country. The party elects the leader, and for that reason the first responsibility of the leader is to the party.

As leader of the Progressive Democrats, I am the main spokesperson for the party. My job is to communicate our message to the people. I have to work to get our candidates elected and I have to make sure our policies are implemented in government.

Decisions are taken democratically in the party – the leader is not a dictator! But the party members are very interested to know the leader's views on issues and

democracy

Ministers from both sides of the Irish border sit down at the first North–South ministerial council meeting

expect the leader to bring up ideas and initiatives. So, the leader has a lot of special responsibilities that only she or he has.

What have you done that you are most proud of in your political life?

I believe that the policies that the Progressive Democrats have implemented in government have led to jobs and prosperity in Ireland like never before. Ireland used to be seen, by ourselves and others, as a failure. Now we have created success, ending mass unemployment and emigration. I am very proud of this achievement.

I am also very proud of the fact that the government I was part of from 1997 to 2002 negotiated the Good Friday Agreement, which received the overwhelming approval of the people in a referendum. The people have said they want an end to past divisions and violence. This is a great achievement in which we all share.

What is the main job of an Tánaiste in government?

The Tánaiste is effectively the deputy to the Taoiseach and is the second most senior member of the government. The Constitution sets out the legal role of the Tánaiste to act in the place of the Taoiseach if he or she is absent or incapacitated or dies in office (until a new Taoiseach is elected).

In coalition governments, like the present one, the Tánaiste is usually the leader of the second-largest party in government. She must work with the Taoiseach in a partnership to make sure that the two parties in the coalition reach agreement on all issues. Their job together is to make sure that the coalition stays an effective, collective government.

Would you encourage young people to become involved in politics and how?

I encourage young people very strongly to become involved in politics. It's very important that we care about how things are done, about our society and our country. And if you care, you should get involved.

Protesting is one way of making your voice heard. Can you think of other ways?

There are many ways of getting involved in politics. The one I know best, and would recommend, is to join a political party whose policies you agree with and whose people you admire and respect.

It's important not just to protest, but to be able to put policies in action.

There are other ways to be involved in politics too, such as joining campaign and community groups. Many people find that satisfying, and many also work in political parties at the same time.

I'd say, whatever you're ready for, join it and get involved. You'll understand your community and your country better and you will find that you can influence things.

 Activities

1.   What does Mary Harney think politics is about?
2.   How does she describe the work she does as a leader of a political party?
3.   What two achievements does she feel especially proud of?
4.   Where is the legal role of the Tánaiste set out?
5.   How does she suggest young people can become involved in politics?

Study 31 An Independent TD Speaks

Read the following interview with Independent TD Marian Harkin and discover how she got interested in politics and why she thinks it is important that young people are interested in politics.

How did you become interested in politics?
I worked in a voluntary role with local community groups. Then I became involved at county level through the Leitrim Core Group of Developing the West Together.

Later I became involved at regional level through the Council for the West and the Western Development Board. A year before the European Elections in 1999 I discussed running with a few friends and family and decided to just 'do it'. Neither my family nor myself have a party political background whatsoever. I realised that, while local and regional

Mary Harkin, TD

groups could make the case and lobby, very often hard political decisions were needed to move the process forward.

Why did you choose to run as an Independent?

Ninety-five per cent of my supporters wanted me to – anyway I am an Independent and I did not enter the political process with the view that party politics was the only road. I believe Independents have an important role to play both at local and national level and can focus on the major issues that affect their constituents while at the same time having a national vision. I do not see anything wrong with party politics but I felt that remaining an Independent was most appropriate for my constituents and me.

How and why do you think young people should get involved in politics?

Become involved locally first in various community and voluntary projects, that is, become political with a small 'p'. Familiarise themselves with issues they consider important, both local and national.

Young people should get involved, as we are talking about the society they will live in.

- Will they have access to training and education when needed?
- Will they be able to get a hospital bed when needed?
- Will there be good quality and affordable childcare available?
- Do you want to live in a racist society and how can your politicians help to ensure this does or does not happen?

Individuals do matter – votes come in ones, not in batches of tens or twenties, and they all add up to give the overall view of the electorate. DON'T be left out because if you don't vote that exactly is where you will be – outside the loop – and finally, don't expect politicians to deliver all you want – they are just part of the picture and another part of that picture is you.

Activities

1. How did Marian Harkin's political career start?
2. What did she become known for promoting?
3. Why did she choose not to become a member of a political party?
4. What does she mean by becoming political with a small 'p'?
5. Why does she say individuals matter?

Study 32 An Interview with a Senator

Read the following interview with Senator David Norris and discover how he thinks young people can bring about change.

How did you become involved in politics?

I was in Trinity with Mary Robinson, who is a friend of mine. She decided to run as a candidate for the Senate election about thirty years ago. She asked me for support, which I willingly gave. My involvement in her campaign showed me that it was one way of getting involved in politics. The idea presented itself to me that this would be a way of first of all circulating my ideas with influential people and secondly it was one of the few ways that I, as a gay man, might get into a position of influence in order to try to correct discriminations in this area. However, my interest very rapidly started broadening out to other areas of injustice.

Senator David Norris

What issues are of particular interest to you?

My interests include human rights and discrimination of all kinds on the basis of race, colour, creed, sexual orientation, etc. I am also particularly interested in the whole matter of foreign affairs and foreign policy and was instrumental in getting the establishment of the Foreign Affairs Committee of both houses for the first time in this country.

Do you think young people should be interested in politics?

Yes, I certainly think young people should get involved in politics. Politics is about the way in which we lead our lives and affects every aspect of our being. Politicians are just ordinary people who take on an extra level of responsibility on behalf of the community. If young people do not get involved decisions will be made about their lives over which they will have no control. It is therefore in their interests to get involved.

How can young people bring about change?

Young people can bring about change by joining lobby groups like the Tibet Support Group, the East Timor Ireland Solidarity Committee, Amnesty International and so on

law

or by joining political parties in the youth section, by voting, by informing themselves about relevant issues and expressing their views in public.

People coming together to campaign about one issue of concern in Ireland – racism

What do you think is the greatest challenge facing Ireland today?

The greatest challenges that face Ireland today are how to maintain our prosperity first of all, and also how to make sure that we share this prosperity with greater equality not only in our own society but by making an input into global politics.

Activities

1. Why did David Norris get involved in politics?
2. Name two issues that he is interested in.
3. Why does he believe young people should be interested in politics?
4. List three ways that a young person can bring about changes named by David Norris.
5. According to David Norris, in what way can we make Ireland and the wider world more equal?

3

Study 33 Making Law

The main job of government is to put laws in place that protect or improve the lives of Irish citizens. Before a law is made it has to go through a series of stages.

Look at the following diagram to see the different stages a law goes through.

STAGE 1	A **bill** is introduced to the members of the Dáil. TDs debate and question what is written in the bill.
STAGE 2	Suggestions and changes are made about what should be in the bill.
STAGE 3	**The Committee Stage** Each part of the bill is examined and any changes are discussed in detail.
STAGE 4	**The Report Stage** Suggested changes are added to the bill.
STAGE 5	The bill goes back to the Dáil with the new changes and is discussed further. No more changes can take place now. The bill goes to the Seanad to be discussed. Bills can be introduced in the Dáil or the Seanad. If a bill started its life in the Dáil it now goes to the Seanad. If a bill started its life in the Seanad then it goes to the Dáil at this stage. Bills *must* go through *both* houses. When the bill gets to the other house stages 2 to 5 are repeated.
STAGE 6	The bill is signed into law by the president.
STAGE 7	The bill becomes an **act**.

law

The **Employment Equality Act, 1998** and the **Equal Status Act, 2000** are two examples of laws that went through the above stages. Under the Employment Equality Act, for example, you are guilty of **discrimination** and you are breaking the law if you refuse to give somebody a job because of any of the following:

- age
- disability
- race
- religious beliefs
- gender
- family status
- marital status
- membership of the Traveller community
- sexual orientation.

Discriminating against people with disabilities is illegal

Under the Equal Status Act, 2000, for example, if you refuse to serve someone in a shop or pub for any of the reasons mentioned above you are also guilty of discrimination and are breaking the law.

The following article shows how these laws have had an effect.

Ryanair fined £8,000 for ageist ad

Ryanair has been fined £8,000 for breaching equality law by advertising a job for a 'young and dynamic professional'.

The £8,000 judgement against the airline is the first successful age discrimination case in Europe and the first taken here under the 1998 Employment Equality Act.

Equality Authority chief executive Niall Crowley said the decision represented the 'casual and accepted discrimination experienced by older people in the workplace'. The authority took the case after Ryanair refused to amend their advertisement, claiming that 'young' implied a state of mind rather than the actual age of applicants.

The £8,ooo will be donated to an organisation which combats ageism.

(*Aideen Sheehan,* Irish Independent)

1. What is the main job of the government?
2. What is a bill?
3. How does a bill become an act?
4. Name one law that went through all the stages and say what this law is concerned with.
5. Why was Ryanair fined?

Study 34 The Law

The **Garda Síochána**, the **Law Courts** and the **Defence Forces** are the means by which the country protects its citizens. Laws are the important rules of the country and like school rules they are there to protect people and property. If you do not obey these rules you are breaking the law. If the gardaí believe a person has broken the law then that person is usually taken to court. The court then decides if the law has been broken.

Garda training at Templemore College

The Garda Síochána

The **Department of Justice** is responsible for the gardaí. There are nearly 11,000 gardaí in the country, most of whom are unarmed. On a day-to-day basis gardaí are involved in such things as responding to calls for assistance in instances of house burglaries, traffic accidents, disputes between neighbours, domestic violence and under-age drinking.

In recent years special units within the gardaí have been set up to deal with the specific problems that our society faces, e.g. the Drugs Unit. Within the gardaí there are also special sections like the Forensic Science Laboratory, which is important in solving murders.

At work in the Garda Forensic Laboratory

law

Crime prevention through schemes such as **Neighbourhood Watch** and **Community Alert** give better protection to people living in isolated and rural areas. A TV programme like *Crimeline* shows how citizens can help the gardaí with crime detection. It asks us as members of the community to become involved where possible.

Interview with a Detective Garda

Read the following interview with Detective Garda Cathal Delaney to find out about the work of the gardaí and how the public can be involved.

Why did you want to become a garda?

When I got the letter saying that I had been accepted to the Garda College, Templemore I had just been offered another good job. It was a difficult decision to make and at very short notice. I decided to go to the Garda College and become a garda because I wanted a challenge, I wanted experiences that were going to change my outlook on life and I wanted to serve the community.

How do you see the work of the gardaí as being important?

The work of the gardaí is important because they provide many services to the public. Gardaí do not only enforce the law to protect life, property and the State. They also do things like visit victims of crime, give advice on preventing crime, work with the public in community policing and many other initiatives.

We live at a time when people expect good service in shops, restaurants and pubs and they also expect it of gardaí. The way that individual gardaí provide services affects how the public see them and how willing they are to assist gardaí. This applies to every type of work the gardaí do: in uniform, as detectives, as administrators or as technical experts. The work of the gardaí is to provide a service that satisfies the public.

What is involved in the work you do as a detective?

My work involves investigating crime. This begins by finding out what crime has been committed, then making enquiries and taking statements to discover who was involved, how they committed the crime, where they did it, when it was committed and why.

When all this information is gathered suspects are arrested and interviewed about the crime. Then a file, a document containing all the evidence and enquiries that were made, is sent to the Director of Public Prosecutions who decides if someone should be charged in relation to the crime.

Do the public play a part in the work of the gardaí?

Policing in Ireland is done with the consent of the public, it is one of the principles that An Garda Síochána was founded on. This is why we don't have armed uniform gardaí.

The gardaí rely on the public to report crimes, to act as witnesses and to co-operate in the investigation of crimes. They are the providers of information that make our job possible. This means each member of the public, from the person begging on the street to the highly paid citizen living in an expensive house, can and do contribute.

I was working in the station one night and it was coming up to the end of my shift. I got a phone call from a very distraught woman saying that her brother had just broken some windows in her house. I listened to her carefully, taking down details as I did. She described the man to me and told me she thought he was still in the area. I got on the radio and sent out the description to all the gardaí on foot patrol in the area and to those in patrol cars also.

Some time later I saw a man walking up the station yard towards the office. I went to the window to see what he wanted and just as he came in the door I saw he matched the description the woman had given me over the phone. I opened the door from the station to the public office and before I could approach him the man said 'I've come to hand meself in, I'm after breaking me sister's windows.' I arrested and charged him.

A traffic garda at work

This is one case where I could definitely say the public were unusually helpful.

This story also shows the dual role that gardaí play in dealing with the public. Our goal is to protect life, property and the State but in doing so we sometimes have to stop people from doing what they want. This can be just stopping a driver who is going too fast and giving him a speeding ticket or it can be arresting someone for having a gun.

law

In order to protect the public we have to be sure that those among them who may cause harm by doing what they want are not allowed to do so. This is the other side of how the public, as wrongdoers, play a part in the work of the gardaí.

Activities

1. What kind of services does Detective Garda Delaney say the gardaí provide to the public?
2. How does he go about investigating crimes?
3. Who finally decides if a crime suspect will be charged with a crime?
4. What actions taken by the public help the gardaí in their work?
5. What does Detective Garda Delaney mean when he says that the gardaí have a 'dual role'?

The Courts System

Laws are made by the government to protect the citizens of the country.

- **Criminal law** is when a person is charged by the gardaí with an offence, e.g. robbery, assault or murder.
- **Civil law** is the law of the state used for civilian and private matters. If someone feels they have been wronged and wishes a court to decide on the issue, civil law is used. Simple examples of such cases might be where a person who has fallen on the wet floor of a supermarket takes the owner to court to sue him or her for the injury caused by the fall and seek compensation. Another example could be a person unhappy with a holiday who takes the travel company to court, claiming that their accommodation was not of similar standard to the one advertised in the company's brochure.

Depending on the type and seriousness of a crime it will be held in one of the following courts.

Court	Case
Children's Court ● There is no jury. ● Cases are held in private.	Minor crimes committed by children under sixteen years of age.
District Court ● There are twenty-three District Courts. ● A defendant could face a fine of €1,270 and/or up to two years in prison. ● There is no jury.	Hears minor cases such as road traffic offences, driving without insurance, theft and some forms of assault. This court can award damages up to €6,350 in civil cases.
Circuit Court ● There are eight Circuit Courts. ● This court has a judge and a jury.	More serious criminal cases are heard here, e.g. assault and burglary. This court can award up to €38,000 damages in civil cases. It also hears appeals from the District Court.
High Court ● Criminal cases are heard here (by the Central Criminal Court, which is part of the High Court). ● There are seventeen judges and a jury system.	Very serious cases like murder, manslaughter and rape are heard here. The High Court can award unlimited damages in civil cases. It also hears appeals. An example of a civil case that might appear in this court would be where a mother, on behalf of her child, sues a hospital for damages that have occurred at birth.
Special Criminal Court ● Three judges. ● No jury.	Often deals with cases relating to the Offences Against the State Act, which includes membership of an illegal organisation, e.g. the IRA. Hears cases where it is felt that the ordinary courts are inadequate.
Court of Criminal Appeal ● Not less than three judges. ● No jury.	It hears appeal cases from the Circuit, Central Criminal and Special Criminal Courts. The case itself is not reheard but the appeal is based on the evidence given at the original trial.

Court	Case
Supreme Court ● Five judges, if the case being heard is a constitutional matter. ● No jury.	It hears appeals from the High Court. No appeal against a decision of the Supreme Court can be made, except when a question of European law, which is more important than Irish law, arises. The president may refer a bill to the Supreme Court before it is signed into law to make sure it does not go against the Constitution. The Supreme Court will make a decision on this.

If a person is unhappy with the decision made by a court, then that person can appeal the decision in a higher court. In an **appeal** a judge looks at a case again and decides whether to change or keep the original decision.

The Defence Forces

The Irish Defence Forces are made up of:

⊕ The Army
⊕ The Air Corps
⊕ The Naval Service

The main function of the Defence Forces is to ensure the security of the Irish state and its citizens. It does this in a number of ways.

⊕ The Army often provides protection for the movement of monies to and from banks.

The Army serving on protection duty

The Naval Service patrolling the waters around Ireland

⊕ The Naval Service gets involved in search and rescue and anti-drug patrols.
⊕ The Air Corps is also involved in many search operations.

The Irish Defence Forces are also involved in many United Nations peacekeeping missions. On p. 163 you can read former Captain Tom Clonan's experience of such missions.

3

⚙️ Activities

1. How does the country protect its citizens?
2. Why do you think people respond to programmes like *Crimeline*?
3. Write a short drama sketch based on the situation below, where the victim meets the criminal.

The Air Corps involved in a search operation

Crime

A cheat 'fixed' the books of the company he/she worked for. Thousands of euros were deposited into the cheater's own bank account. The company went bankrupt as a result of this. All the staff were made redundant. The victim has been looking for a new job for nearly a year.

The Cheat

- Is an accountant
- Lives in an apartment
- Drives a BMW 5 series.

The Victim

- Was an employee at the same company as the cheat, but is now unemployed
- Has a nice home but is getting into debt
- Is married with four small children.

The criminal might explain why he/she committed the crime and the victim might describe how the crime has affected his/her life. Your short sketch could then be acted out in class.

Survey: Do a survey of people your age to find out their views on crime. The survey could ask questions like:

- Do you know what crimes are most common in your area?

rights and responsibilities

- Have you or has anyone you know been a victim of crime?
- Do you feel safe in your home and locality?
- How do you think crime could be reduced?

Your classmates or the students from another class could answer the questions in your survey. You could present the findings of your survey as a wall chart or newspaper article.

Issue Tracking: Look through local or national newspapers and see what types of crimes are most frequently reported. You could invite a solicitor/barrister/garda/army representative to your class to explain their work.

Study 35 Influencing the Government

A person does not have to be a member of a political party or the government in order to influence decisions made at national level. People who want to take action on a particular issue often join local or national groups that are concerned with that issue.

Organisations, sometimes called **interest groups** or **pressure groups**, try to persuade politicians to take their ideas and concerns into account when making decisions. Some organisations, such as the **Irish Farmers' Association**, are concerned about the interests of their members, while others promote a cause, such as the **Irish Society for the Prevention of Cruelty to Children**.

Farmers taking part in a protest march

Pressure Groups

Pressure groups try to influence the government by means of lobbying. Lobbying could mean:

- writing to a local councillor or TD
- getting people to sign a petition
- organising a demonstration or protest, perhaps outside the Dáil or a local council office
- contacting the media by preparing a press release
- seeking interviews on radio and television.

The advertisement on the next page was placed in several Irish newspapers by an organisation called **Focus Ireland**, which is a voluntary organisation concerned with the needs, rights and welfare of people who are homeless in our society. This advertisement is one example of how interest groups **lobby** the government and try to influence public opinion.

 Activities

1. What issues are Focus Ireland concerned with?
2. How do you think this advertisement could put pressure on the government?
3. In what other ways might an organisation like Focus Ireland influence government policy?
4. Imagine you are forming a pressure group over some issue that concerns you, such as an environmental issue or a service you need in your community. How would you go about persuading other people (public opinion) and the government to take your point of view into account?

The Budget

Government departments and ministers can take the concerns of pressure groups into account when they are deciding what changes they will make or what new projects they will create.

Announcing the budget

Ministers then go to the Minister for Finance and argue their case for more money so that these changes or projects can be achieved.

When all the government departments have agreed how much they will spend in a year, the Minister for Finance announces how the government will raise the money to pay for everything. This happens on budget day, when the Minister for Finance makes the budget day speech in the Dáil.

People are usually interested in what the government proposes at this time because money to run the country – to provide good hospitals, health services, a good education system and

democracy

WHILE OUR POLITICIANS CANVAS DOOR TO DOOR, SOME PEOPLE HAVE TO SLEEP IN THEM.

A cruel reality.

We see it everyday. Homeless children, women, men and families. It's so hard to understand how we allow it to happen. We want to do something but we don't know where to start.

And these are only the most visible homeless people. Countless others whom we never see are homeless also.

As our politicians canvas to be elected to Leinster House, Ireland is in the middle of a housing crisis. A chosen few will be elected and have the responsibility to do something about the 140,000 people on the housing waiting lists who urgently need a proper and secure home. People who may be only one lost job, large bill or broken relationship away from losing their existing address.

"We qualify for local authority housing but there are 750 applicants ahead of us on the waiting lists. Myself and my husband pay €800 a month for a one-bedroomed flat. We want to start a family. We want a real home. Though we have a roof over our heads, I'd say we're homeless."
Margaret, 27, living in rented accommodation in Dublin .

Apart from those living in insecure and unsafe accommodation, Focus Ireland estimates that there are at least 6,000 people who are homeless. Everything is temporary in their lives. They cannot make plans for the future as they are moved from place to place. They become isolated. They lose any real sense of belonging. Living on the streets or in cramped emergency accommodation, children have nowhere to play and often no-one to play with.

"My son keeps asking me: 'Ma when we will have a proper home?' I can't answer him. It breaks my heart. I can't even plan where to send him to school next year as I don't know where we'll be living by then. "
Mary 26, homeless and living with her partner and child in emergency accommodation in Dublin.

This is Ireland's real housing crisis. Thousands of people who wait the long wait, not knowing when or where they'll be able to secure what's rightfully theirs – a permanent place to call home.

"It takes most families I work with at least 16 months to get a permanent house from the local authorities and it takes single people even longer. Maybe a few years. The right housing and services still aren't there for many other people with additional problems."
John O'Hare, Crisis Worker, Focus Ireland.

"How can my son start school in Autumn when home is a B&B?"

There has been a dramatic rise in the use of B&Bs as emergency accommodation for homeless people in Dublin – from 5 to 1200 in 9* years – despite the government admitting that this form of accommodation is unsuitable.
* 1990-99

Human rights begin at 'home'

Ireland has responsibilities under international legalisation which guarantees housing as a basic human right. Focus Ireland believes it is shameful that we are failing to live up to these responsibilities. Existing policies alone will not prevent it becoming an even worse crisis. Meanwhile a large part of the solution to homelessness and the housing crisis is glaringly obvious – more social and affordable houses. This must be a key priority of the next government. A non-negotiable target. We cannot stand by any longer and allow our citizens to be treated so callously.

Building a solution.

The real scandal is that homelessness and the housing crisis can be solved. If our politicians decided there were votes in it, more dynamic action would be taken and the problems could be minor ones inside ten years. It would just take some hard decisions, proper resources and a creative approach. But it would also take one other simple thing – Real Commitment. That's why every voter must ensure that every vote they give in this election is also a vote against homelessness. We ask you to raise these issues with all politicians currently canvassing your support and ask them what they plan to do about them.

Focus Ireland – Helping to build a solution

Focus Ireland provides over 250 people with a place to call home in our housing developments in Dublin, Limerick and Waterford. We also provide practical help and a range of services to people who are homeless or at risk of becoming homeless.

Focus Ireland is one of the leading organisations working to combat homelessness and the housing crisis. We believe everyone has a right to live their life with dignity so we work to raise awareness of the many complex problems of homelessness and to influence future government policy in this area. In the past two years alone our research has revealed some shocking facts:

● A massive jump of 33% in people contacting our crisis service as they're been evicted from private rented accommodation and made homeless.

● 50% of homeless children are at risk of contracting infectious diseases because of incomplete or no immunisation. *

● 25% of the parents of homeless families were homeless themselves as children.*

● A rise of nearly 10% last year of people sleeping rough getting help from Focus Ireland

● Over 66% of young people leaving Health Board care in Ireland experience homelessness within the first two years.   * Pilot Study

Just do two things

1. **Retain this page and keep it accessible near your front door.**
2. **When canvassers call, question them on the 3 actions below.**

3 Priority Actions for the new government.

1 Legislate for a Right to Housing. Housing is a basic human right. The next Government must take action to meet our international obligations that guarantee a right to housing and also legislate to remove the inequalities in the Irish housing system.

2 Integrated and comprehensive strategies must be adapted by all local authorities to effectively address homelessness:
● No children and families should be forced to live in B & B accommodation.
● There must be appropriate outreach and settlement services & facilities for people leaving care.
● Single adults who are homeless must be provided with suitable accommodation.

3 Urgent action must be taken to effectively cut the housing waiting lists.

Focus Ireland will monitor the record of the new government on dealing with these crucial problems. We will continue to work hard for justice and fairness. Focus Ireland also urgently needs your material help as well as your moral support – please send us a donation today to help us continue to push for change, and to provide vital services and housing. Please complete the donation form below or Callsave 1850 204 205 to make an instant donation. Thank you for supporting Focus Ireland in our work helping people find and sustain a home.

Donate instantly by credit card 1850 204 205 or donate online www.focusireland.ie

---

OUR INTERNATIONAL OBLIGATIONS

Article 31 of the Revised European Social Charter (EU) committed all member states to:
■ Promote access to adequate housing.
■ Prevent and reduce homelessness.
■ Make the price of housing accessible to those without adequate resources.
Ireland ratified this charter but refused to consider itself bound by Article 31 stating that: "Ireland is not in a position to accept the provisions of this article".

The International Covenant on Economic, Social and Cultural Rights (Article 11) recognises the right of everyone to an adequate standard of living including housing and that appropriate steps be taken to ensure that right.

FOCUS IRELAND

roads – comes from the citizens of Ireland in the form of taxation. The two most common types of taxes are:

- **Direct taxes**, which means that if a person is employed money is taken directly from their wages or salary.
- **Indirect taxes**, which means that the government adds a tax on items purchased. Usually these are on luxury goods such as petrol, cigarettes or alcohol.

If people did not pay tax there would be no money to pay for the services that we all need.

 Activities

1. What is budget day?
2. Make a list of items that you think are luxuries.
3. Sometimes difficulty arises between the government and the people if the government raises the amount of tax a person is to pay. Suggest reasons why this would cause conflict.
4. Imagine a scene in which the Minister for Finance is having a meeting with some colleagues. Can you identify from the list below which minister would say what? Example: A = 7.

X	1	2	3	4	5	6	7	8
Y								

Y

A. 'I need more money to control pollution.'
B. 'I need more money for schools.'
C. 'I need more money to help create jobs.'
D. 'I need more money for Irish-speaking areas.'
E. 'I need more money for prisons and the gardaí.'
F. 'I need more money to help small farmers.'
G. 'I need more money for the Air Corps and Naval Service.'
H. 'I need more money to encourage more visitors to come to Ireland.'

X

1. Minister for Education and Science
2. Minister for Enterprise, Trade and Employment
3. Minister for Arts, Sport and Tourism
4. Minister for Community, Rural and Gaeltacht Affairs
5. Minister for Justice, Equality and Law Reform
6. Minister for Agriculture and Food
7. Minister for the Environment and Local Government
8. Minister for Defence

democracy

ACTION

Role-play: Imagine you have been given €200 to spend on some aspect of your school, e.g. improving your school grounds, developing the sports facilities, upgrading the canteen or recycling school waste.

- Elect a class member as Minister for Finance.
- Elect two class members who will act as senior civil servants to advise the minister.
- Divide the rest of the class into groups. Each of these groups decides what they would spend the money on and why, as well as how they would raise more money for their project.
- Each group presents its case to the Minister for Finance and his/her advisors.
- After hearing all the ideas and arguments the minister and the advisors decide which project should go ahead on the basis that it is the most needed in the school and also the most practical.

If you come up with a very good idea you might present it to your principal.

In chapter 2 you saw how communities can come together over a specific issue that affects their area, like the lack of facilities for young people. People and communities also come together and interact with national government over issues that all are concerned about, but can have different views on. Sometimes communities challenge decisions made by national government, and in other cases they work with national government to come up with the best solution for all concerned.

Study 36

Case Studies - In Action with the State

The following case studies show how different communities try to create change with the aid of various state agencies.

State agencies are bodies set up over the years by various governments. They are formal structures that try to help with employment and the development of our resources. Examples are:

- **An FÁS** (the Training and Employment Authority) – this was set up to provide training and employment programmes and to support community-based enterprise.
- **An Bord Fáilte** – this was set up to promote tourism in Ireland by providing grants (money) and marketing services.

- **Combat Poverty Agency** – a state agency working for the prevention and elimination of poverty and social exclusion. The agency's job is to advise policy-makers about the best ways to tackle poverty and bring about a fairer society.

The case studies show how different communities are trying to tackle issues that are of concern to them and national government.

Read **one** or more of these case studies and see how people can work in **partnership** with, or challenge, government.

law

Case Study 1 – Moy Valley Resources

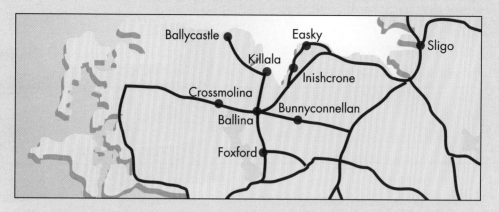

Moy Valley Resources is a local development company operating in north Mayo and west Sligo.

Unemployment was a problem in the area. Some fifty-two per cent of those unemployed were long-term unemployed (i.e. they were out of work for twelve months or more).

It was against this background of high unemployment and high emigration that Moy Valley Resources was formed by a group of local people. The company set down what it wanted to do. They wanted to:

- create jobs
- create economic development
- enhance their environment
- promote opportunities in tourism, agriculture, food and small enterprises (businesses).

To achieve this the company developed programmes in several different areas. The whole operation is being financed by FÁS and other state agencies, as well as by local contributions.

Here are some of the programmes that have been put into operation.

Community Development

Local communities were shown what grants and national programmes were available to help them put their ideas into action:

- a visitor centre at the Foxford Woollen Mills was created

- the Easkey Surfing and Information Centre was built
- the Ballina Salmon Festival was started up again.

Environmental Development

The aim of this programme is to make the area more attractive to locals and visitors alike.

- derelict houses have been fixed up
- the railway station in Ballina has been restored
- many green areas have been landscaped

Much care has gone into improving the appearance of the Moy Valley area

- each village has its own enhancement programme and they work in partnership with the county council, Tidy Towns committees and community groups. They are put into effect with the help of FÁS Community Employment Schemes and volunteers.

Tourism Development

Moy Valley Resources has produced literature and video material to market the area abroad and to increase the number of tourists visiting the area. With the aid of the Leader Programme* the following tourist projects have been created:

Waterpoint is the Aqua Centre at Inishcrone, Co. Sligo

- an equestrian centre
- an emigration museum
- seaweed baths have been started or improved
- Aqua Centre, Waterpoint, in Inishcrone.

> * The Leader Programme is a mainly EU-funded programme that gives grants and advice to help rural development.

development

All these developments are run by and employ people from the local communities.

According to Mr Billy Lewis, chief executive of Moy Valley Resources, their success has depended on 'the community believing that they can win and overcome. The community owns every project in every village itself.'

Mr Lewis also believes that the success has been due to 'the great working relationship with various state agencies, allowing the people of the area to fully develop their potential and the resources in the region.'

 Activities

Case Study 1

1. Why was Moy Valley Resources started up and by whom?
2. What are the aims of the company?
3. Give one example of development in the following areas:
   - environmental development
   - tourism development.
4. Give examples of assistance that came from outside the community.
5. What reasons does Mr Billy Lewis give for the success of this company?

Case Study 2 – Partnerships

Community development, employment and education programmes are some of the areas that local partnership boards* throughout the country are interested in.

Ballymun Partnership is concerned with employment and enterprise, education and childcare and they work in partnership with other groups and organisations like FÁS and Dublin Corporation to achieve greater benefits for local people.

AXIS, Ballymun's new Arts and Community Resource Centre, is the first community facility to be completed in the regeneration of Ballymun. The centre came from the need to house the activities of the many arts and community development organisations within Ballymun. 'Kick Up The Arts For Ballymun' is how the Ballymun Partnership announced an initiative to get feedback from the community on how people would like their new arts centre developed. It set up shop in a unit in Ballymun Shopping Centre and invited people to give their views on video, on tape or by drawing, painting or in a questionnaire.

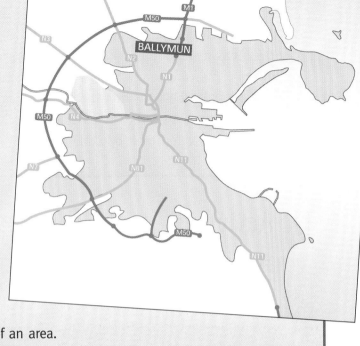

Sean Cooke, chief executive officer, says that AXIS is a good example of what can happen when the local community, state agencies and other key funders work in partnership for the benefit of an area.

André Venchard, a local resident employed in the centre, says that AXIS gives him the chance to work in a creative environment in his own community and to add to the on-going development of the centre. 'The challenge for me is to help create a place where I would like to spend time on my own days off as well as working here.'

Ballymun Arts and Community Resource Centre

The Ballymun Arts and Community Resource Centre has a 220-seat theatre, a second performance space, a café bar, recording and rehearsal studios, a crèche, conference facilities, training rooms and community offices.

* Partnership boards involve trades unions, employers, government agencies and community groups coming together to bring about employment and community development.

democracy

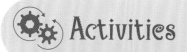

Activities

Case Study 2

1. What groups and organisations make up a partnership?
2. Name two areas Ballymun Partnership is concerned with.
3. How did Ballymun Partnership get the views of local people on the new arts centre?
4. Do you think partnerships are a good idea? Give reasons for your answer.

Case Study 3 – The Burren Action Group

Sometimes decisions made at national level are challenged by the people of the State. It may happen that a government or State body takes an action that some citizens disagree with. The following case study is an example of such a situation.

The Burren in County Clare is a limestone landscape that has been internationally recognised because of its huge range of flora, fauna and rare habitats. The area was seen as being so important that the State Wildlife

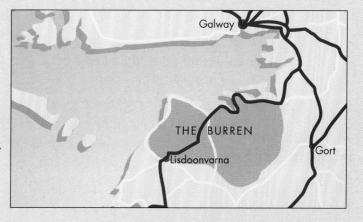

Service recommended that it should become a nature reserve.

Ten years ago the government announced plans to establish a National Park in the south-west region of the Burren. It also announced plans to build an interpretive centre in the heart of this area.

While the people of Clare welcomed the plan for a National Park, many were concerned about the site chosen for the interpretive centre on the grounds that such a centre, which would bring many visitors each year, would damage the delicate environment of the area.

As a result a public meeting was called to discuss this fear that a core area would be destroyed and the entire Burren area threatened by development. From this meeting the Burren Action Group (BAG) was set up. Those involved included local farmers, teachers, craftworkers, people without jobs, labourers and doctors. These people were mostly from west Clare.

Their main aim was to campaign for the relocation of the interpretive centre to a more suitable site in or near a village on the edge of the Burren, which they felt would be more able to cope with the expected numbers of visitors.

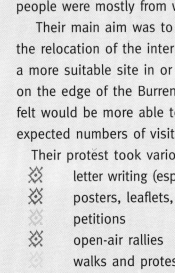

The Burrens's limestone landscape is famous for its wealth of flora and fauna

Their protest took various forms:

- letter writing (especially to newspapers)
- posters, leaflets, fliers
- petitions
- open-air rallies
- walks and protests at the site of the proposed development

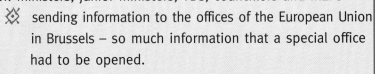

U2 support the Burren Action Group

- lobbying (i.e. speaking to) everyone they could think of: ministers, junior ministers, TDs, councillors and MEPs
- sending information to the offices of the European Union in Brussels – so much information that a special office had to be opened.

The poet, Seamus Heaney, is a supporter of the Burren Action Group

Support for their viewpoint came from almost all environmental groups in Ireland, including the Irish Wildlife Federation and Earthwatch, as well as many concerned individuals like Eamon de Buitléar, Seamus Heaney and members of U2.

Despite their campaign, work on the site continued and was only stopped by High Court and Supreme Court civil action taken by the group. Five years later, a new government announced that the ➡

planning application for the interpretive centre would be withdrawn and that the partially completed development on the site would be taken down.

However, the government then announced plans for a 1.5-acre car park and the construction of a 110-square-metre building as an entry point to the Burren National Park. The Burren Action Group continued its fight. The new plan was eventually rejected by An Bord Pleanála. The Minister for the Gaeltacht, Arts, Heritage and the Islands then got legal advice. After getting legal advice the government accepted that the partly completed development on the site was illegal and that the site must be restored to its previous condition. After nine years the Burren Action Group's fight was over. However, the financial cost to the members of the group who took action was very high.

After the announcement by the minister that the site would be restored some local residents who were not in agreement with the actions of BAG put up signs at the site saying 'Save our Car Park'. In most campaigns there will be different viewpoints on an issue.

 Activities

Case Study 3

1. Why did some people in Clare decide to set up the Burren Action Group?
2. What kind of people got involved in this action?
3. What was the main aim of their campaign?
4. What kind of protests did they carry out?
5. Who did they lobby?
6. Name some of the organisations or well-known people who supported their cause.
7. What action did they take to stop the building on the site?
8. After getting legal advice what did the government have to do?
9. Why do you think some local residents would want the building to go ahead?
10. Imagine you are going to attend a public meeting about this issue and address the audience. Write out your speech, outlining your arguments for or against the building of an interpretive centre.

Case Study 4 – Kathy Sinnott v the State

This case study is an example where an individual citizen, Kathy Sinnott, challenged the State over the provision of education for her son.

Jamie was a beautiful normal baby who quickly and easily gained the early baby skills, but at four months his development was disrupted. He lost his skills and screamed constantly. The doctors who examined him decided that he was disabled and that his family should take him home and watch the disability develop.

Kathy Sinnott

Jamie needed help and needed it quickly. There was no early intervention available so his mother, Kathy, took him to Chicago. He was diagnosed with autism and was helped to learn. When he got home there were no services and he regressed. At three years old, Jamie returned to Chicago and made progress, even speaking his first word. This time, Kathy was assured that services would be in place for Jamie when she brought him home. They weren't and Jamie again regressed.

In looking for an education for Jamie, Kathy discovered that the Department of Education had a policy of excluding severely disabled children from school on the basis that they were 'ineducable'. Kathy wrote to government departments, the Health Board and lobbied politicians. With a group of parents, she started two groups to campaign on behalf of children and adults all over the country who are refused an education and other vital services.

With the passing of years Jamie's level of disability became profound.

In 1993, the O'Donoghue Judgment confirmed that the Irish Constitutional right to free primary education applied to all. Three years later Jamie, now eighteen years old, had his first full day of school. However, when he was nineteen, he was told that he must leave school, as his education was complete. Kathy took his case to the High Court.

During a four-month trial, Judge Barr listened carefully to both sides and in October 2000 ruled that the Irish Constitutional guarantee of free primary ➡

development

education was based on need, not age, and that Jamie and others like him were entitled to education for as long as they could benefit.

Jamie began a school programme at home and began to learn. He stopped acting confused and miserable and became hopeful and happy. In the first week of class, he said two words. Despite Jamie's progress, the State appealed the decision to the Supreme Court stating that the right to education stopped at eighteen years. There was public outrage at the State's decision to appeal the High Court judgment.

In March 2001, seven judges heard the appeal. This was the first time the Supreme Court used so many judges. The State argued that adults who needed education would be educated but not as a right. On 12 July 2001, the Supreme Court handed down a decision that there was no constitutional right to education after eighteen years of age. This decision was met with great sadness and anger.

Kathy continues to campaign for persons with special needs and has promised not to give up until they are respected and included in our society.

These case studies show how national issues can be tackled by communities and the people in them, some in partnership with state agencies, using the government as the servant of the people who elect it. The Burren case study is an example of local people challenging decisions made by national government.

National issues are the responsibility of us all, including national government.

 Activities

Case Study 4

1. Why did Kathy Sinnott take Jamie to Chicago?
2. When Jamie was a child, what was the Department of Education's policy towards 'severely disabled' children?
3. What actions did Kathy take about this situation?
4. Why did Kathy take a case on behalf of Jamie to the High Court?
5. What ruling did the High Court make about Jamie's case?
6. How did the Supreme Court ruling change the decision that had been made in the High Court?
7. How did this ruling affect Jamie's case?

Study 37 Ideas for Action Projects

Democracy

1. Invite a TD or senator to visit your class to explain how he/she became involved in politics.
2. Do an interview with a young member of a political party.
3. Arrange a visit to the Dáil or to the Seanad.
4. In groups form your own political parties, presenting your main policies to your classmates. You could run an election in your year group.
5. Hold an inter-class table quiz based on how Ireland is governed.
6. Survey schoolmates or family and friends on their knowledge of Irish politics.
7. Hold an election or referendum in class or school.

National Issues

1. Find out about a national issue you feel strongly about and design an information poster to raise awareness of the issue.
2. Organise a debate about a national issue.
3. Choose an issue and contact political parties to find out about what their policy is regarding this issue.
4. Carry out a survey in your area to find out about attitudes towards unemployment or poverty.
5. Conduct a survey in your school to find out how many of your school friends' brothers and sisters have left the area to find work and where they went.
6. Contact an organisation like ALONE to find out what changes they'd like to see the government make on issues that concern them.
7. Fundraise for an organisation that you feel strongly about.
8. Invite a member from a Partnership Programme/Leader Programme into class and find out about their work.

> Remember to look back over the action ideas that are suggested throughout the chapter for more topics for an action project.
>
> In chapter 5 you will find advice and helpful hints on how to do posters, leaflets, surveys, interviews, petitions and fundraising events.
>
> In the assessment section of chapter 5 you will find a breakdown of exactly what kind of information is needed for all sections of a Report on an Action Project (RAP) and a Coursework Assessment Book (CWAB).

democracy

Study 38 Revision Questions

(Revised Exam Format – 80 Marks)

Section 1 – 18 Marks
Answer ALL questions.

1. Which **two** of the following politicians are also leaders of a political party? Put a tick in the box opposite the correct names. (4 marks)
   (a) Michael Martin ☐
   (b) Bertie Ahern ☐
   (c) Mary Harney ☐
   (d) Mary Banotti ☐

2. Indicate whether the following statements are **True** or **False** by placing a tick beside the correct answer. (4 marks)

	True	False
(a) The ancient Romans were the first people to rule by democracy.	☐	☐
(b) The system of voting we use in Ireland is called proportional representation.	☐	☐
(c) A quota is the smallest number of votes needed to be elected.	☐	☐
(d) In Ireland you can be fined if you don't vote.	☐	☐

3. Fill in the missing words in the following sentences. (4 marks)
   (a) If a person is registered to vote they will receive a _____ _____ in the post a few days before an election.
   (b) People who work for the State are called _____ _____. They are expected to equally serve whichever government is in power.
   (c) The head of the government is called ___ _____ in Ireland.
   (d) The Department of _____ is responsible for the gardaí.

4. In the boxes provided below match all the letters in row X with the corresponding numbers in row Y. The first pair is completed for you. (6 marks)

X	A	B	C	D	E	F	G
Y	3						

X

A. A manifesto is
B. Fianna Fáil is
C. The Constitution is
D. The Seanad is
E. The Labour Party is
F. A State agent is
G. The Dáil is

Y

1. built on the principle of socialism.
2. made up of sixty members.
3. a document produced by political parties saying what they will do if elected.
4. the largest political party in Ireland.
5. made up of 166 members.
6. a book containing all the basic laws of the country.
7. a body set up by the government to help with employment and the development of resources.

Section 2
Answer ALL questions numbered 1, 2 and 3 below.
Each question carries 14 marks.

1. Read the following description of the work of a TD and answer the questions that follow.

At weekends most TDs meet the people of the area they have been elected to represent. The meetings are called clinics; the TD meets people to discuss the problems or issues which they think the TD can help them with.

During the week a TD may contact a local authority which could be of help in solving some of the problems that have been raised at the clinics.

A TD spends most of his/her time in the Dáil dealing with the issues that may be raised at the clinic, and taking part in debates on national issues and proposed new laws. If a TD wants to raise an issue that is important in his/her constituency, he/she usually does this at Question Time in the Dáil.

(a) Name **two** things a TD does in a working week. (2)

(b) List **two** ways a TD might deal with problems raised at his/her clinic. (2)

(c) Describe an issue you could contact a TD about. (2)

(d) Suggest **two** actions you would take in a campaign to raise awareness of the importance of voting in a general election.

Action 1 (4)

Action 2 (4)

2. Read these explanations of poverty and answer the questions that follow.

'The biggest cause of poverty is that we take it for granted. We just accept it as part of life.'

'We have a poverty problem, because people just think of making money for themselves and rarely think of what they can do for others.'

'Poverty needs to be solved by better training and education for young people and adults. We need to give people skills so that they can enter the workforce with confidence.'

(a) List the causes of poverty mentioned in the above statements. (6)

(b) Choose **one** statement you agree with, explain it in your own words and say why you agree with it. (2)

(c) Choose **another** issue that you think is a national issue and explain why you think it is important. **Hints:** transport/housing.

Issue (2)

Why it is important (2)

(d) What action would you take over the issue mentioned above?

Action (2)

3. Look at this photo and answer the questions that follow.

Gorey Echo

Wexford County Council Get the Message

137

(a) What are these people protesting about? (2)

(b) Name **two** other methods of protest this group could have used. (2)

(c) In your own words explain what a pressure group is. (2)

(d) Name an issue that has featured in the news about which people have protested. (2)

(e) State an issue that you feel is important and suggest **two** actions you would take over this issue.

Issue (2)

Action 1 (2)

Action 2 (2)

Section 3
Answer ONE of the questions numbered 1, 2 and 3 below.
Each question carries 20 marks.

1. Imagine that you are part of a local development group. A government agency wants to know why your group should get money for a festival in your area. Write a report that includes the following:

   (a) the sort of events you would hold

   (b) explain how your area would benefit from the festival

   (c) list what forms of advertising you would use to attract people to the festival.

2. Imagine you are the Taoiseach. Prepare a speech you would give on your first day in the Dáil outlining changes that you would like to see made in Irish society.
   Hints:
   ● changes in education/the transport system/the environment/young people working
   ● solving the problem of homelessness.

3. Imagine your CSPE class has decided to invite a TD to your class to outline his/her work.

   (a) Write a letter of invitation explaining to the speaker why he/she is being invited.

   (b) Make a list of all arrangements that would have to be made to ensure a pleasant visit for the speaker.

   (c) Outline practical steps that you could take to share with the wider school community the new information you have about the work your TD does.

 Now test yourself at **www.my-etest.com**

development

04 chapter

SECTION A – IRELAND AND THE WORLD ■ **SECTION B** – DEVELOPING OUR WORLD

In chapter 3 you learned how we as citizens of Ireland participate in and influence what happens at a national level. But as citizens of Ireland we are also members of international groupings such as the European Union and the United Nations. Through our membership of international groupings and by our actions as individuals we participate in and influence the wider world and so have responsibilities beyond our own country.

Study 39 Our Connections to the EU

We do not have to look very far to see some of our **connections with the wider world**. Think about the food you eat, for example, and where it comes from. The cereals you eat were probably grown in the United States, while the jam you eat may come from Belgium, the fruit from Latin America, the tea from India, and perhaps the coffee from Brazil. The tee-shirts you wear may have been made in Bangladesh, the jeans in America. Some of the clothes we wear do not carry a label stating the country of origin because they are made for large chainstores in Europe.

Today there is vast movement of goods around the world. To make this process easier it often helps if countries have trade agreements. This is one reason why we joined the **European Union**.

Activities

1. Name any international fast-food restaurants that you eat in.
2. Can you name some experiences that would be common to many people the world over, e.g. music or sport?
3. Which TV programmes do you watch and where are they made?
4. Name some popular makes of cars that you see in Ireland and say what countries they are made in.

interdependence

Being a member of the EU affects all our lives. Read the following story to see some of the ways the EU can have an impact on your life.

It was CSPE class again and the teacher took us to the computer room to look at a CD ROM called 'Me, You and the EU'. Halfway through, Mr Irwin stopped the CD to tell Jessica to turn around and how she obviously knew all about the EU and would she like to tell the rest of us about how the EU had affected her life.

Mr Irwin thought he was asking a hard question but little did he know how Jessica loved talking, especially about her trip to Spain.

'Sir, when I went to Spain last year I had to get loads of stuff ready, like my passport which had the EU as well as Ireland printed on it. I also got an **E111** form, which my mother wouldn't let me go without because it covers medical emergency attention in any EU state.

'And Sir, not having to change money because of the **euro** was great. It made it easier to figure out how much everything cost. When I was there I visited France and didn't have to go through customs checks crossing the border. I met Pierre there Sir and we . . .'

The class started to giggle and with that Mr Irwin told Jessica that she could stop there. He then asked us all if we could think of any other ways in which the EU had affected our lives or the lives of our families.

Moya put up her hand. 'My older sister, Katie, who's in the hotel business has **worked** in loads of different EU countries from Sweden to Greece without any hassle, she doesn't need a work visa because Ireland is an EU member. Sir, have you ever worked anywhere else besides here?'

Mr Irwin then told us how as a student he couldn't find work grape picking in France so he drove his beat-up old Fiat to Amsterdam and found work in a tulip bulb factory. He said that because Ireland was an EU member his **driving licence** was valid in any EU country.

4

Large road signs show the input of the EU

Jessica put up her hand and said, 'Sir, is that the same Fiat you drive now?'

Mr Irwin grinned and called Jessica 'a right tulip' (whatever that meant). He then asked if anyone else had any examples.

Jamie raised his hand and said, 'My brother is in France, but he's not grape picking Sir, he is studying at a university in Paris as part of the **EU Erasmus Programme**.'

Jamie went on to tell us that his brother liked Paris so much that he decided to live there. Then he was allowed to **vote** for a French MEP in the elections to the European Parliament.

We then all had to think again of any other stuff we'd noticed.

Eva's hand shot up. 'Sir, my granny lives in Dublin and I used to hate travelling up to see her because we always got stuck in Kinnegad, but now with the new by-pass the trip's much shorter. Sir, aren't loads of those **by-passes** funded by the EU?'

The appearance of many farms benefited from the REPs scheme.

Mr Irwin agreed that they were and asked us if we had noticed the signs on new roads that said, 'Funded in part by the EU'. We all nodded our heads.

Sam then butted in telling us how he often went to visit his granddad's farm and that his granddad had got a grant under an EU scheme to improve some farm buildings, clear the farm of litter, and repair fences and stone walls.

Mr Irwin told us that many farms around the country had been improved under this scheme, which was called **REPS** (Rural Environmental Protection Scheme).

With that the bell rang. As we left class Mr Irwin promised us we'd see the rest of the CD the next day. Jessica shouted back, 'I can't wait Sir!'

Activities

1. List six ways that the students in the story show how the EU has affected their lives or their family's lives.
2. What is REPS?

Study 40 The History of the EU

Why a European Union?

After World War II people in Europe lived in fear of a similar catastrophe happening again. Many people thought that the best way to prevent war between European nations was to create strong economies, more employment and a higher standard of living. Leading statesmen, in particular **Jean Monnet** and **Robert Schuman**, felt that if the economies of European countries were linked closer together there would be less chance of war. But how could small European states compete against huge markets like the USA and the USSR? A United States of Europe was their answer.

A Brief History of the European Union

A map of Europe showing the EU member states in 2002

1951

Six European states signed the **Treaty of Paris** and formed an organisation called the European Coal and Steel Community (ECSC). Coal and steel were really important in the rebuilding of Europe after World War II. It was felt that if countries co-operated in the production of these resources it would be difficult for one country to plan a war in secret. The six states were Belgium, the Federal Republic of Germany, France, Italy, Luxembourg and the Netherlands.

1957

The same countries signed the **Treaty of Rome**, which set up the European Economic Community, or EEC. This meant that a 'common market' was created in Europe. Now goods could be traded freely among member states. The idea of the free movement of people, services and money was introduced among member states.

1973

Ireland, the UK and Denmark joined the EEC.

1979

The European Parliament was **elected directly** by the citizens of the EEC for the first time.

1981

Greece joined the EEC.

1986

Spain and Portugal joined the EEC.

1987

The EEC became known as the European Community, or EC. The Single European Act was signed to remove barriers that still existed to free trade.

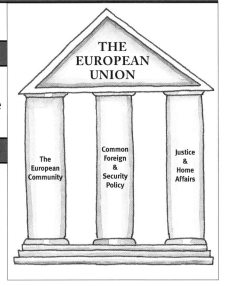

1993

Under the **Maastricht Treaty** countries agreed to:
- introduce a single currency by 1 January 1999
- change the name of the EC to the EU to show that the EU interests itself not just in economic affairs but also political affairs
- introduce the three pillars of the EU.

1995

Austria, Finland and Sweden joined the EU.

1999

On 1 January, eleven EU countries introduced the euro.

The Amsterdam Treaty (sometimes called Maastricht II) broadened many of the areas agreed to in the Maastricht Treaty. One of the main changes that this treaty brought about was that for the first time the EU would take on a military role. It would become involved in peacekeeping, humanitarian missions and peace making or peace enforcement by the creation of a European Rapid Reaction Force.

2000

The Nice Treaty proposed a number of changes to the institutions of the EU to prepare for more countries joining (enlargement). For example, the number of MEPs would increase from 626 to 732, each member state would have only one commissioner and there would be changes to how many votes each country was to have on the Council of the European Union. The EU charter of fundamental rights of all EU residents was also signed in Nice in December 2000.

2001

A **referendum** was held in Ireland and the people of Ireland voted against the Nice Treaty.

2002

On 1 January **euro** notes and coins came into circulation.

A **second referendum** was held in Ireland after the Irish government had a declaration signed by the other EU member states saying that the Treaty would not affect Irish neutrality. This time the Treaty was accepted.

The aim of the European Union is now not only to create closer economic ties but also closer political ties. This will involve a **common foreign policy** and closer co-operation on security matters.

Many other countries have applied for membership of the EU. Within the next ten years the EU could expand to include twenty-five or more states. The combined population of the EU is bigger than the population of the USA. The EU is now the largest trading power in the world.

 Activities

1. Why did Jean Monnet and Robert Schuman want European countries to have closer ties?
2. What are the three pillars of the European Union?
3. Choose one European Union treaty and say what changes it brought about.
4. Find out which countries have applied for membership of the EU.
5. What does being 'European' mean to you?

Study 41 The EU - How it Works

Three important EU institutions are:
- The European Commission
- The European Parliament
- The Council of the European Union.

A triangular relationship exists between the Commission, the Parliament and the Council.

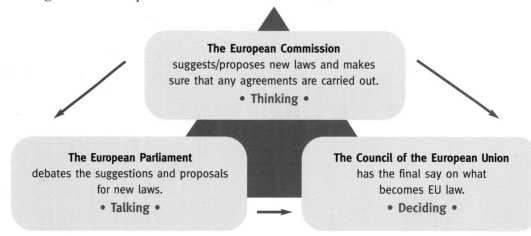

The European Commission
suggests/proposes new laws and makes sure that any agreements are carried out.
• Thinking •

The European Parliament
debates the suggestions and proposals for new laws.
• Talking •

The Council of the European Union
has the final say on what becomes EU law.
• Deciding •

The European Commission

The Commission is appointed by national governments, not directly elected by the people. The Commission and its administration are based in **Brussels**. Its main functions are:

- To propose new laws and send them on to the Parliament and the Council.
- To make sure that decisions made by the council are carried out. If they are not they can refer cases to the European Court of Justice.
- To administer the EU budget.

The European Parliament building in Strasbourg

The European Parliament

The Parliament is the only body **directly elected** by the citizens of Europe. The number of MEPs that represent each country is based on the size of the population of that country.

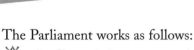
United in democracy

They serve a five-year term of office. Currently there are 626 members of Parliament. With enlargement the Parliament will increase in size and the number of Irish MEPs could be reduced from fifteen to twelve.

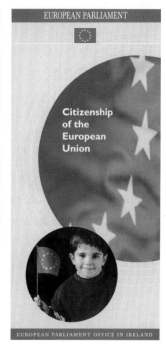

The Parliament works as follows:

- the Commission passes on ideas for new laws to the president of the Parliament
- the president of the Parliament sends these proposals to one of the twenty committees set up to deal with different issues like the environment and education

The full sitting of the European Parliament

* the Committee(s), meeting for two weeks every month in Brussels, prepares reports on these proposals for new laws
* a full meeting of the Parliament in Strasbourg debates the reports.

MEPs elected from Ireland or other member states do not sit together as a national grouping in the European Parliament. Each MEP joins one of the **nine political groupings** within the Parliament which most reflects the ideas of his/her own national party, or stays as an Independent.

The main functions of the Parliament are:
* to help make community law
* to approve or reject the budget each year
* to supervise the work of the Commission and the Council
* to give its agreement before any new country can join the EU.

It also has the power to dismiss the Commission, which it has done.

Pat Cox MEP, president of the European Parliament 2002–200[?]

The Council of the European Union *(the Council of Ministers)*

The membership of the Council changes according to which topic is under discussion. If, for example, the environment is being discussed then the Ministers for the Environment from the different member states will get together. So at any meeting of the Council, no matter what the topic, each country including Ireland will be represented. The Council of the European Union and its administration are based in **Brussels**.

Its main functions are:
* to make the final decision on what becomes community law
* to consult with the Parliament on new laws suggested by the Commission.

The Presidency of the Council of the EU

Every six months the presidency changes. Each EU country takes its turn.

The job of the presidency is:
* to organise and chair meetings
* to discuss policy issues that are causing difficulty in the EU
* to try and find solutions to these problems.

Summit meetings are also held by the country that holds the presidency. These meetings happen

democracy

about twice a year and are attended by heads of national governments and the president of the Commission. They discuss difficult or controversial issues faced by the EU, e.g. deciding on a common foreign policy.

 Activities

1. How many more MEPs has Germany than Ireland?
2. Can you name any Irish MEPs?
3. What stages does a proposed law have to go through before it reaches a full sitting of the Parliament in Strasbourg?
4. What is the job of the Parliament?
5. What is the job of the Council of Ministers?
6. What are Summit meetings?

ACTION

Research: Do a survey to find out how much your friends and family know about the European Union. You could use the information in this chapter to decide what questions should be asked; ten to twenty questions should be enough. You could then present your findings as a report or a graph.
Sample question: What is the term of office of a MEP?
(a) 5 years   (b) 7 years   (c) 10 years

Discussion/Essay: The idea of a European superstate is a good one.

Study 42 EU Budget - EU Funds

Who Pays for the European Union?

Common Budget

GOING IN
Every member state has to give money to the EU every year.

GOING OUT
Spent on agriculture, environment, training, technology, etc.

The EU cannot go into debt. A special body called the European Court of Auditors makes sure that the money is spent properly.

During the twenty-five-year period up to 1997 Ireland contributed £6 billion to the EU budget and received £27 billion back. For every €1.27 we were giving we were getting nearly €6.35 back. This money has been given to us through a series of different funds which aimed to reduce the wealth gap or economic difference between us and richer EU states like Germany and France.

These funds include **Structural Funds** used:
- to help unemployment
- to develop roads
- to give guaranteed prices to farmers for their products
- to modernise the fishing industry
- to provide money for training and education.

The amount of money Ireland has received under Structural Funds will greatly decrease over the next few years. Irish farmers will see a drop in guaranteed prices for their produce (beef, milk, cereal) under reforms in the CAP (Common Agricultural Policy).

European Community Humanitarian Office – Echo

Echo is the world's largest donor of **humanitarian aid** and provides funding to aid agencies like the Irish Red Cross, Trócaire, Goal and Concern to help them to do their work. Echo is based in Brussels. About 5.1 per cent of the EU budget is spent this way.

Activities

1. How has Ireland benefited from the EU funds?
2. Suggest the advantages and disadvantages of having a single currency/euro.
3. Can you think of any groups in Irish society that have not benefited from our improved economy? Give reasons for your answer.

ACTION

Interview: Find out from a local farmer about how EU grants and policies have affected his/her profession and way of life.
Hints: REPS scheme, CAP.

Study 43 Ireland and Issues in the EU

Prague, the capital of the Czech Republic

Some issues that Ireland and other member states are concerned with are the questions of **enlargement**, refugees and the **security** and **defence** of Europe.

Enlargement of the EU (more countries joining) has major implications. Money will have to be put aside to develop the economies, infrastructure (roads) and agriculture of many of the Eastern European countries wishing to join. Countries that have received large sums from the EU budget, like Ireland, will no longer be entitled to the same level of funding. In May 2004, when Ireland has the presidency of the EU, the following countries will join: the Czech Republic, Estonia, Latvia, Lithuania, Poland, Hungary, Slovakia and Slovenia, as well as the two islands of Cyprus and Malta.

As the European Union co-operates more in the areas of **security** and **defence** the question of **Irish neutrality** is becoming more of an issue. Ireland is not a member of the following military organisations.

- ⊕ **WEU** (the Western European Union) aims to achieve more unity in the areas of defence and security. However, Ireland can send a representative to attend and speak at meetings of the WEU.
- ⊕ **NATO** (North Atlantic Treaty Organisation), a military alliance of European states, Canada and America.

NATO troops are drawn from European and North American countries

Under the Irish Constitution, joining in a common defence could only happen if the people agreed to it in a referendum. Some argue that being neutral allows Ireland to make positive contributions to world affairs, as what we say is considered to be an independent viewpoint. Ireland is not influenced or obliged to take the lead from larger nations or international military organisations.

However, others argue that Ireland cannot 'sit on the fence' when it comes to matters of defence and security.

There are also many social issues which member states are concerned about. These range from racism and landmine disposal to health and food issues, road safety and the environment.

⚙ Activities

1. Why is enlargement an issue in the EU?
2. What are WEU and NATO?
3. Do you think Ireland should be a neutral country?
4. Which European issues would be of concern to you? Give reasons for your answer.

ACTION

Research: Investigate the countries that have applied for membership of the EU.

- You could present your findings in map form.
- Present a brief history/profile on these states. Note the population of these countries, as these will give you an indication of how much say they will have in a larger EU.

Study 44 How You Can Influence the EU

There are many ways in which citizens of the EU can influence events in Europe.

1. You can **petition** the European Parliament by sending a written request or complaint to the Parliament. For example, the Parliament has received many petitions urging it to take a stance in the areas of **human rights** and **environmental protection**. It was because of numerous petitions received on animal welfare that the European Parliament pushed harder to make EU laws to cover these issues.

2. You can **contact** your local **MEP** to raise issues that concern you.

3. Once you are eighteen you can **vote** in European Parliament elections. If you decide to live in another EU country, you will have the right to vote in their local and European elections. You would also be able to stand for the European Parliament in another EU country.

4. You could **bring a case** to the **European Court of Justice** if a national law that affects you contradicts an EU law.

Petition the EU

Read the following article to see how one Irish woman made use of the petitions committee of the European Parliament.

The EU produces many information leaflets like this

Kerry Roads Group Takes its Case to Brussels Committee it Found on Internet

The petitions committee of the European Parliament will hear a submission in Brussels tomorrow from the West Kerry Roads Action Group on the condition of the N86 between Tralee and Dingle.

The chairperson of the group, Ms Brigid O'Connor, lobbied local TDs for more than a year in an effort to have something done about a road that is meant to be one of the main tourist routes in the State but which, in effect, is a nightmarish collection of twists, turns and potholes.

When all else failed, Ms O'Connor searched the Internet and discovered the little-known petitions committee and that she could make her case for a hearing by filling in an electronic form. She was backed by villagers from

West Kerry Roads Action Group stop traffic at Blennerville, 2 June 2002, as they launch a flyer asking tourists to support their campaign to upgrade the N86 Tralee/Dingle road

Camp, Annascaul, Castlegregory, Cloghane and The Maharees who formed the action group.

The committee responded last June, telling the group their case was admissible and that they would be notified of a date for the hearing. Tomorrow eleven members will fly out from Shannon to Brussels. They believe the case will finally receive the attention it never got at home.

It was new territory to her, Ms O'Connor said yesterday, and the Internet search was a last resort. 'But it paid off and they're going to hear what we have to say. I will have five minutes to make an oral submission but they already have our written one.'

The core of the action group's case is that Kerry is the fourth-largest county in Ireland but only ranks fourteenth in the pecking order for road funds.

She believes the committee will want to know why this is so and will ask the government to give an account of how European funds are dispersed. There may be some red faces, she says.

Kerry County Council says it would cost about €21 million to tackle the N86 and it doesn't have the money.

(*Dick Hogan*, The Irish Times)

Activities

1. Before going to Brussels who did the chairperson of the action group lobby?
2. What does Ms O'Connor think is wrong with the road from Tralee to Dingle?
3. How did Ms O'Connor find out about the petitions committee?
4. What is the 'core' of this action group's case?
5. Why does Ms O'Connor think there 'may be some red faces'?
6. What does Kerry County Council have to say about this issue?

Other Petitions

Another petition that the committee received was from a European citizen whose parents died on a holiday in Spain. The apartment they were staying in had very little ventilation and was fitted with a gas-fired shower unit. These units are common throughout Europe but are not used in Ireland.

democracy

The lack of ventilation together with the gas-fired shower unit caused these two people to die from carbon monoxide poisoning. The two sons complained that the hospital in Spain would not release the records of their dead parents.

The **petitions committee** investigated this matter and found that several other people had died in the same apartment complex. Further investigations also showed that sixty-three people in Belgium had died from the same cause and that the deaths, which had been put down to over-eating and drinking, were in fact caused by carbon monoxide poisoning from these shower units.

The petitions committee of the European Parliament receives thousands of petitions each year.

The European Court of Justice

The European Court of Justice sits in Luxembourg and is made up of fifteen judges appointed for a six-year term. Any individual, company or EU country can bring a case to the court. Sometimes it settles

A sitting of the European Court of Justice, which is held in Luxembourg

disputes between member states or between a member state and the European Commission.

The court is extremely important because its decisions are final and take priority over, or are more important than, the decisions of national courts. The court has the power to request a member state to change any law that is not in keeping with EU law and to impose a fine on any member state that fails to do so.

Here is a case that was brought before the European Court of Justice.

Soccer has become an increasingly popular sport. It is interesting to note that FIFA, the world soccer governing body, has 209 member countries, while the UN has only 189 members.

> The case concerned the freedom of movement of workers. It occurred when a Belgian footballer, Jean-Marc Bosman, wanted to transfer from his club RC Liège to US Dunkerque, a team in the French Second Division, because they were offering him a better contract (more money).
>
> When he was prevented from doing this he took his case to the European Court of Justice. The court said the UEFA ruling limiting the number of foreign players on a team went against the principle of the freedom of movement of workers in the EU, so Bosman won the right to transfer for himself and all other football players in the EU.

4

Activities

1. Write a letter to a MEP over an issue that concerns you and that you want them to take action on.
2. Imagine you are standing for election to the European Parliament. What reasons would you be giving people to vote for you? Explain your answer.

Study 45 Interview with an MEP

Read the following interview with Brian Crowley, MEP and discover why he became involved in politics and what his life as an MEP is like.

How did you become involved in politics?

My father was a politician, and when he retired from politics I kept up the involvement with the Fianna Fáil party as a member of the organisation. I helped out during elections and suggested strategies and policies. Later when I stood for election I truly believed that we needed to have more young people involved in politics to ensure that the attitudes of fifty per cent of the population would be represented in the European Parliament, and also to try and bring forward new ideas on how we could improve our country and our society.

Brian Crowley, MEP

What would a typical month be like for you?

Each month is divided into the four weeks. Monday to Thursday of each week I am abroad as part of my work in the European Parliament. Three weeks are spent in Brussels where the committees of the Parliament meet and the fourth week in Strasbourg where the plenary sessions take place. That is, the full 626 members of the European Parliament meet to take the final debates and votes on issues which were dealt with in the committees in the previous weeks in Brussels. Also, I deal with the European Commission and the Presidency of the Council, putting questions to them on urgent topical issues on international, national or local levels. Each Friday, Saturday and Sunday I am back home in my constituency of Munster meeting with different groups of people and dealing with their problems as well as talking with them and discussing Europe and issues that they have concerns about.

rights and responsibilities

Why do you think the European Parliament is important?

The European Parliament is important because it is directly elected by the people in Europe every five years. Each region of every country has the right to elect its own representative on the wider European scale and to act as a public representative in voicing their concerns, promoting their areas and ideas and ensuring that there is a connection between decision-making at a European level and the people in their own homes.

Activities

1. Why does Brian Crowley believe that we need to have more young people involved in politics?
2. Why does he spend three weeks of each working month in Brussels and one week in Strasbourg?
3. What work is he involved in at weekends?
4. Why do you think Brian Crowley mentions the importance of there being 'a connection between decision-making at a European level and people in their own homes'?

Study 46 The United Nations

The United Nations was set up on 24 October 1945, after World War II. This day is now celebrated around the world as United Nations Day.

The UN building, New York

The main aims of the UN are:
- to keep peace throughout the world
- to develop friendly relations between nations
- to encourage respect for each other's rights and freedoms (see UN Declaration of Human Rights p 8)
- to help people live better lives by solving the problems of poverty, disease and illiteracy in the world, as well as trying to put a stop to environmental destruction.

All actions by the UN depend on the will of member states to accept, fund or carry them out.

4

How the UN Functions
The Security Council

- The main aim of the Security Council is to keep **international peace**.
- It meets in New York.
- It has **fifteen members. Five of these are permanent**: France, China, Russia, UK and USA. The other ten are elected by the General Assembly.
- It has the power to take decisions which member states then carry out. However, any of the five permanent members can stop an action or decision happening even if the other fourteen are in favour. **This is called the power of veto**. For this reason the Security Council has not always been successful in taking action in crisis situations.

Kofi Annan,
Secretary General of the UN

The General Assembly

- The General Assembly is the closest thing to a world Parliament; nearly every nation of the world is a member (189 members at present).
- This is where the member states can discuss any matter of global concern.
- Every member has **one vote**, regardless of the size of the country.
- It encourages co-operation between different countries and the protection of human rights.
- When the General Assembly agrees on an issue it is known as a **resolution**. However, these decisions or resolutions cannot be enforced.

Secretary General

- The Secretary General acts as the head of the United Nations.
- He/she carries out the decisions made by the Security Council.
- He/she acts as a mediator (go-between) in conflict situations.
- He/she is the head of the civil service of the UN (secretariat).

The United Nations organisation has a number of special agencies that depend on money from member states to achieve their goals.
Special programmes include:

United Nations Children's Fund

- UNICEF – United Nations International Children's Emergency Fund
- UNHCR – United Nations High Commissioner for Refugees
- UNEP – United Nations Environmental Programme

interdependence

- WHO – World Health Organisation
- UNAIDS – United Nations Agency dealing with the AIDS epidemic

Changing Times at the Security Council

The Security Council of the United Nations usually meets to discuss crisis conflict situations around the world, but in January 2000 the first topic on the agenda was HIV/AIDS in Africa. The Security Council had never before dealt with a health issue.

Public health information, education programmes and expensive drug treatments which have helped to contain the HIV/AIDS situation in the developed world are beyond the reach of many countries crippled by debt. In Africa HIV/AIDS is linked to poverty.

At the end of the year 2001, an estimated forty million people worldwide were living with HIV.

In the Masaka district of Uganda a grandmother aged seventy, who lost every one of her eleven adult children to AIDS, was left looking after her thirty-five grandchildren. One in four families in Uganda are now looking after an AIDS orphan.

However, not all are fortunate enough to have someone to look after them. According to Dr Peter Piot, executive director of UNAIDS, many AIDS orphans end up roaming the streets. They are prime targets for gangs and for creating more child armies, like those that participated in massacres in West Africa.

This is why the UN had to put AIDS in Africa at the top of its list of priorities in order to look at possible solutions to the problem.

 Activities

1. What is the aim of the Security Council?
2. Why is the Security Council sometimes not successful in taking action?
3. What is the General Assembly?
4. Who is the Secretary General and what does the job involve?
5. Do you think human rights education is important? Give reasons for you answer.

UN Goodwill Ambassadors

There are now 100 Goodwill Ambassadors chosen by various UN agencies. Kofi Annan has said 'the Goodwill Ambassadors have the power to inform people about the hardships of others and do something about it . . . putting their names to a message could break through the barriers of indifference and lack of news coverage . . . they could explain how the UN changed people's lives, strengthened peace and ensured human rights.'

Can you name these Goodwill Ambassadors?

Some Goodwill Ambassadors include Angelina Jolie (actress), Geri Halliwell (singer), Seamus Heaney (poet), Magic Johnson (basketball player), Ronaldo (footballer), Muhammad Ali (former heavyweight champion) and Michael Douglas (actor).

Mary Banotti, Irish politician, is also a UN Goodwill Ambassador. Read the following account of her work as a UN Goodwill Ambassador with the UN Population Fund. UNFPA is concerned with mothers' (maternal) health and the health of their newborn babies. Every year over half a million women die in childbirth worldwide.

In Afghanistan a huge number of mothers die having their babies because there are very limited services available. Many babies are born on the floor of whatever dwelling the mother is in, usually the floor of mud huts. Surprisingly, the babies are a very good weight. I went with a particular view of women's lives in Afghanistan under the burqa. I expected to find them downtrodden and weak. I was enormously encouraged; the women of Afghanistan are mad for education. It struck me that these women will be an enormous influence in their country with relatively little help. I was delighted to see after their tribal meetings when they came to elect the leader of their country, Mr Kasan, that the main challenger was a woman.

I visited a new school for married women. A lot of the women look a lot older: that is because of the difficulty of their lives and the number of children they have. In this school the women were all there with their copy books doing science. The school provides places where the children can be minded while the mothers are in school. Our interpreter was a

Under the Taliban women had to wear a traditional garment called a burqa

democracy

fourteen-year-old boy of one of the women who had English. They are all desperate for education.

I was invited by the UN to become a Goodwill Ambassador. Our job is to help with the work of the United Nations. I am one of two politicians among all of the UN Goodwill Ambassadors. In a sense, I have a particular role in terms of my influence with politicians. I'm more experienced in that line than many of the other ambassadors. Geri Halliwell and Angelina Jolie are UN Goodwill Ambassadors too. We were all in the UN this week; Mr Annan invited us all there. We had two days of meetings discussing general issues. We came to the conclusion that that we'd be more effective if the UN Goodwill Ambassadors for the different agencies, like UNICEF, WHO, UNFPA, etc., worked together.

The job is voluntary, we are not paid and I intend to continue with this work I hope for many years.

Refugees in Afganistan

Women in a World of Difference

	Ireland	Afghanistan
Women dying in childbirth	1-2 per year	2 per hour
Infant mortality *(per 1,000 births)*	6	161
Birth rate *(per woman)*	2	6.9
Life expectancy	79.6	43.5
Girls in primary education *(enrolled)*	100%	8%

(Source: UNSPA and Department of Health)

Model United Nations Conferences for Secondary Students

In order to understand how the UN works a number of model United Nations Conferences take place around the world each year. In Ireland St Andrew's College in Booterstown, Dublin hosts a conference every Easter with up to 800 Irish and foreign students taking part.

Each group of four to six students takes on the role of a country and becomes an expert on that country and its different policies. Each student delegate joins different committees where questions relating to the environment, human rights, etc. are discussed. In these

Irish students at the Model United Nations Conference

4

discussions the student delegate puts forward the viewpoint of the country they represent. The aim of the conference is to get as many resolutions (recommendations for actions to be taken) as possible passed in the model General Assembly. Part of the process is that student delegates have to lobby other student delegates in order to persuade them of their point of view.

The Methodist College in Belfast also runs a Model United Nations Conference each year.

 Activities

1. According to Kofi Annan, how can the UN Goodwill Ambassadors help the work of the United Nations?
2. The majority of the ambassadors are celebrities. How can they draw attention to the work of the UN?
3. What was Mary Banotti surprised by on her trip to Afghanistan?
4. What school did she visit?
5. How can Mary Banotti's experience as a politician help her in her work as a Goodwill Ambassador?
6. How does the Model United Nations Conference help students understand the workings of the United Nations?

ACTION

Research: Find out more information about the United Nations. Here are some examples to help you:

● find out what work the UN does in the area of human rights
● find out about the work of one of the UN's special agencies.

 Study 47

~

The Irish army is involved not only in the security of the State but also as part of the United Nations peacekeeping missions. Irish Defence Forces have been involved in UN peacekeeping missions since 1958 in places such as the Lebanon, Somalia, Bosnia, Kosovo and East Timor. The differences between UN peacekeeping forces and other armed forces are:

⊞ UN peacekeeping cannot take sides
⊞ countries involved must agree to the presence of peacekeepers

- UN peacekeepers are generally lightly armed and only use arms in self-defence
- UN peacekeepers are also involved in clearing mines, providing humanitarian aid to local people, investigating human rights abuses, and observing and reporting on a situation as well as monitoring elections when necessary.

The most basic principle is that using arms and force is not the best way of solving a conflict. Peace will last only when there is some form of agreement.

The following interview with former Captain Tom Clonan describes the kind of work carried out by the Irish Defence Forces.

Why did you join the Defence Forces?

I chose the army as a career for many reasons. I wanted a job that was not limited to the normal nine-to-five routine. As an army officer, my work is varied, active and often outdoors. Having command of troops demands a high level of commitment. The army offers many training and educational opportunities as well as the opportunity to work with other organisations, such as the Garda Síochána and other armies.

Irish UN peacekeeping forces on patrol

What tour of duty did you do as part of a UN peacekeeping mission?

I served overseas with the UN in South Lebanon. I served a six-month tour of duty in a village called Al Yatun with the 78th Irish Battalion. The tour involved conducting day and night patrols, monitoring and reporting on incidents involving resistance groups and the Israeli Defence Forces. During the tour we experienced heavy shelling and machine and rocket attacks.

During the trip we gave much humanitarian assistance to the local population and especially to the orphanage in the village of Tibnine. This aspect of the trip was certainly the most satisfying. I also spent two months in Bosnia in the former Yugoslavia. I worked in the Serb-held area of Prijedor and helped in the monitoring of local elections.

UN forces in Bosnia

How have the Irish Defence Forces helped the international community?

The Irish Defence Forces are the world's seventh-largest contributors of troops to the UN. We have been involved with the UN since 1958. In that time we have gained a considerable reputation as excellent peacekeepers. I believe this is due to the Irish temperament and our communication skills. We are well respected in many trouble spots and are seen as being independent in disputes.

However, it must also be remembered that the Defence Forces play an important role in the security of the State along with the Garda Síochána. This has included border patrolling, prisoners' escorts, cash escorts, explosives escorts and bomb disposal. The Defence Forces are now considered world leaders in the area of bomb disposal and train teams from the international military community.

 Activities

1. Give two differences between a UN peacekeeping force and other armed forces.
2. Name three activities that Captain Clonan has carried out as part of a UN peacekeeping mission.
3. Why do you think he found giving humanitarian aid so satisfying?
4. According to Captain Clonan, why are Irish peacekeeping forces well respected?
5. Describe some of the work the Defence Forces do at home.

Interview: You could invite a member of the Defence Forces who served abroad to speak to your class about their experience of a UN peacekeeping mission.

interdependence

Being members of the wider world means that we are members of a broader community. In the previous chapters you saw how being a member of a community brings with it certain **duties and responsibilities**. Being a member of the world community, the global village, means that every individual, especially those in positions of power, has a responsibility to show concern for those who are without power.

Study 48 Child Labour

Children as young as five years of age are working to earn money in countries such as India, Bangladesh and the Philippines. In total there are more than 250 million children between the ages of four and fifteen who are working. Many are leather workers, carpet weavers, tea pickers, brick makers, farm workers and workers in garment and toy factories, who produce many of the products that end up in our shops.

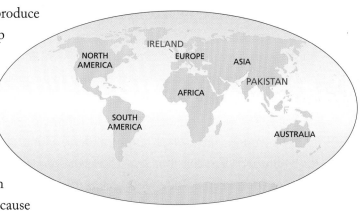

Many of these children work because their families are poor. Their parents may be out of work or so badly paid that the family needs all the extra money that the children can possibly earn. Sometimes, because families need money for basics like food and clothes, parents sell their children into **bonded labour,** which means that they receive a sum of money and the child must work to pay off the loans. This can go on for life.

Employers can save money by using child workers.

- child workers earn as little as 38–51 cent a day
- children are less likely to know their rights and form trades unions to organise for better pay and conditions.

Children who work from a young age suffer many hardships:

- they work long hours, often up to fourteen hours a day
- they have little time for rest or play
- they work in cramped and unhealthy conditions
- some work with dangerous chemicals and fireworks, without protective clothing.

Children who are forced to work are **denied their basic rights**. They have little time to play. They cannot go to school. As a result they will not be able to find better jobs when they grow up and so their children will also have to work to survive.

 Activities

1. Explain what 'bonded labour' means.
2. Give two reasons why employers use child labourers.
3. What hardships might child labourers suffer?
4. Look at the Convention on the Rights of the Child (p. 9) and name some of the rights that child labourers are being denied.

The following tells the story of Iqbal Masih, a child labourer.

Iqbal Masih lived in the village of Muridke in Pakistan. His family was extremely poor and lived in a two-roomed hut. When Iqbal was four years old, his family was given a loan of 800 rupees (about €12.70) in return for putting Iqbal to work in the village carpet factory. Some 500,000 children aged between four and fourteen work in carpet factories in Pakistan. They work for fourteen hours a day. These children are considered good workers because their small hands are good for tying the knots of expensive hand-knotted carpets.

These child workers receive no formal education. They are not allowed to speak during working time in case they make mistakes in the patterns. They have one thirty-minute lunch break per day and are often forced to work overtime without extra pay. Complaints result in punishments such as beatings or having their hands plunged into boiling water.

Iqbal was extremely unhappy at the carpet factory but his parents could not afford to have him set free. One day Iqbal heard the founder of the Bonded Labour Liberation Front (BLLF) speak about their work in freeing bonded labourers and about new laws which forbade child labour. Iqbal asked how he could be set free. He knew the factory owner claimed that his parents now owed 16,000 rupees. He was afraid that his entire life would be spent repaying the debt. He wanted to have a childhood like other children.

When Iqbal returned to the factory, he told the owner of his rights and stated that he would no longer work as a slave. The carpet master was furious and punished him severely, but still the child refused to work. Iqbal said, 'I am not afraid of the carpet master. He should be afraid of me.' The factory owner demanded his worker or his money. The family could not convince Iqbal to work and so the factory owner threatened them.

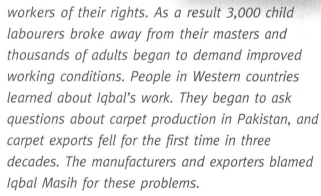

The family had to flee from the village. Iqbal was taken by the BLLF to a school. He was ten years old and worked very hard, quickly learning to read and write. He hoped that one day he could become a lawyer helping to free child labourers.

When he was eleven years old, Iqbal began to work with the BLLF. He snuck into factories to see where the child labourers were kept. He began to make speeches at the factory gates telling the workers of their rights. As a result 3,000 child labourers broke away from their masters and thousands of adults began to demand improved working conditions. People in Western countries learned about Iqbal's work. They began to ask questions about carpet production in Pakistan, and carpet exports fell for the first time in three decades. The manufacturers and exporters blamed Iqbal Masih for these problems.

Iqbal was given a number of human rights awards and invitations to visit a number of Western countries. Doctors in Sweden found that he was the size of a child half his age. He suffered from tuberculosis (TB), his spine was curved and his fingers bent by arthritis.

Why do you think children are used in carpet making in some countries?

167

On his return Iqbal found that the BLLF was in trouble. Threats of violence had been made against BLLF's workers and teachers.

In April 1995, Iqbal went on a visit to Muridke to see some members of his family. As he travelled with a cousin through fields near the village, a shot rang out and Iqbal Masih fell dead. A poor labourer confessed to the killing but later withdrew his confession. International pressure has failed to get any satisfactory answer as to why Iqbal Masih, aged thirteen, died.

It is widely believed that he was killed for his work fighting child slavery.

The publicity that Iqbal's story received meant that a global campaign on child labour in the carpet industry grew. The **RUGMARK label** is your best assurance that no illegal child labour has been used to make your carpet or rug. RUGMARK works to get rid of child labour in the South Asian carpet industry through factory monitoring, consumer labelling and educating and training former child labourers.

The RUGMARK label is your best assurance that no illegal child labour has been used

The RUGMARK Foundation gets carpet producers and importers to make and sell carpets that are free from illegal child labour. These producers then receive the right to put the RUGMARK label on their carpets.

 Activities

Iqbal's Story

1. What happened to Iqbal as a result of his family's poverty?
2. What kind of conditions did the children work in?
3. Why did Iqbal begin to think about being set free?
4. What do you think Iqbal meant when he said, 'I am not afraid of the carpet master. He should be afraid of me'?
5. What were Iqbal's hopes for the future?
6. What effects did Iqbal's speeches at the factory gates have on the workers?
7. What did people in the West do when they heard Iqbal's story?
8. How did the denial of Iqbal's needs and rights affect him physically?
9. Why do you think Iqbal was killed?
10. What does the RUGMARK label mean?
11. When human rights are abused in other places in the world and we hear of them, what actions can we take?

rights and responsibilities

Study 49 The Debt Crisis

The developing world consists of much of Asia, Africa and South America. It is also referred to as the **South, Third World** or the **Majority World**. The grinding poverty experienced in many countries in the developing world, where the basic needs and rights of people are not met, is due in part to the debt these countries owe.

In the 1970s the price of oil rose, making lots of money for oil-producing countries. A lot of this money was put into Western, or First World, banks. Bankers wanted to earn more from this money so they offered loans to Third World countries at low interest rates.

The loans went to countries in South America, Africa and Asia. These loans were often used to try to rapidly industrialise Third World countries rather than develop agriculture, on which most people's living depended. **Many of the loans never reached the people they were intended for** because of corruption. Some of the large schemes that received loans were very questionable. For example, a nuclear power plant was built in the Philippines at the foot of a volcano in the middle of the Pacific earthquake zone. The project cost $2.1 billion. According to *The New York Times*, the then president of the Philippines, President Marcos, received $80 million commission from the company that was contracted to build the plant. However, other countries did put the loans to good use. For example, Tanzania invested money in health and education programmes.

The amount of money these countries had to repay was increased when global interest rates rose. International organisations like the World Bank insisted that Third World countries cut back on government spending in order to repay their debts. This meant that health and education programmes were cut, keeping people who had no part in the arrangement of these loans in poverty.

Patients awaiting care in Zimbabwe

- In the developing world ten million children die each year from malnutrition and easily preventable diseases such as diarrhoea.
- In the developing world 1.3 billion people have no access to safe drinking water.
- In the developing world over one billion adults cannot read or write.
- In the developing world about 800 million people do not get enough to eat.

The World Bank admits that for every €1.27 spent on aid to the Third World €11.43 is spent by these same countries to pay their debt.

In a world which each year spends $28 billion on golf and $200 billion on smoking, a mere $6 billion would provide access to primary education for all those children who currently do not receive it.

The debt crisis also affects the people in First World countries, as we are all **interdependent**. In First World countries the effects of world debt can be seen in many ways.

- The **global environment** is affected when natural rainforests are destroyed and replaced with cash crops grown for export in order to earn money for debt repayment.
- The **drug trade** increases as many farmers in developing countries stop growing crops such as coffee and cocoa because world markets are unstable. Instead, they grow drug crops to earn money. The effects of drugs can be seen in many First World communities.
- The debt crisis is adding to the number of **immigrants/displaced people** around the world as people move to try and escape the trap of poverty.

Many groups and individuals, such as **Jubilee 2000**, have been calling on the World Bank, the International Monetary Fund and large creditors such as Germany, France, Japan and the USA to cancel the debts of the poorest nations in the world. The worldwide campaign to cancel the unpayable Third World debt has had some success. By January 2000, $110 billion was cancelled from the approximately $354 billion owed.

At the start of the campaign many believed that the cancellation of debt was unwise and impossible. However, through pressure and lobbying change happened. In Ireland alone, 800,000 people signed the Jubilee 2000 petition campaign. **People-power worked**.

US Senator Richard Lugar and Bono promoting the Jubilee 2000 campaign

The responsibility for these debts is a heavy burden that falls on the peoples of these nations, as Dominga de Velaques of La Paz in Bolivia explains.

> 'And we the housewives ask ourselves: What have we done to incur this foreign debt? Is it possible that our children have eaten too much? Is it possible that they have studied in the best colleges? Have our wages become too great? Together we say: No, no, we have not eaten too much. No, we have not dressed any better. We do not have better medical assistance. Then to whom have the benefits gone? Why are we the ones who have to pay for this debt?'

The cancellation of the debt is a positive step and will go some way to improve the lives of millions of people throughout the world.

Data

Bono from U2 has set up a new lobbying or pressure group called **Debt Aid and Trade for Africa** (DATA). Bono believes that many First World countries like the USA are not convinced that giving aid to Africa will change the situation or make life better there. He has set out to make world leaders change their minds.

Bono in Africa with US Senator Paul O'Neill

Read the following extract of a speech given by Bono at an African Development Bank meeting.

> 'This is where it all started for me. Seventeen years ago, I came to Ethiopia on a wave of tears flowing from the rich countries to the poor, from soccer stadiums taken over by musicians to refugee camps taken over by the starving war-weary people of Ethiopia. The brilliant Bob Geldof taught me then the importance of being focused, angry . . .
>
>   We raised $200 million and we thought we'd cracked it. It was a great moment, a great feeling. Then I discovered that Africa pays $200 million every five days repaying old debts. Can I repeat that, $200 million every five days. Tears were obviously not enough.

The problems are complex, nobody denies that; we've seen it with our own eyes.

But there are a few big decisions that we simply can't wait on any longer – three million people in this beautiful country are walking around with the death sentence of HIV on their heads. That's as many people as live in my home of Ireland. The AIDS epidemic is acting as the wake-up call for us all around the world, to put excuses and old attitudes behind us.

So what can we do?

First, it is not acceptable that these countries are still servicing old debts. It is not acceptable that Ethiopia, where sixty-two per cent of adults cannot read, where one million children are orphans, is paying $100 million to us – this is not acceptable at any level, any where, any how.

Many people in the developing world cannot afford medicines that would save their lives

Second, of course we are looking for an increase of aid. We need to put billions more in, and we must see it for what it is: value for money, smart money for the United States and Europe, because the chaos that will ensue if we don't will cost us a lot more in the long run. Look what happened when we abandoned Afghanistan.

When aid works, it really works. Money is not going down a rat hole as a few people have said in London and Washington. It is more likely to be going down a water hole. Saving children from dying of diarrhoea, guinea worm, water-borne killers.

It is an investment. It is an investment we can't afford not to make, in the most valuable resource of all – people. But as the new African leadership knows, aid by itself is not the answer.

Because, thirdly, these countries need to be allowed to trade fairly. Not free trade: fair trade.

Activities

1. What other Irish person is mentioned by Bono and why?
2. What is the 'wake-up call' Bono talks about?
3. Name the three things Bono says can be done to help Africa.

Other factors that block human development in many developing countries include:

- excessive spending on weapons and armies
- reduction in natural resources like rainforests
- rapid urbanisation (people moving from the country to cities).

The Progress of Man

1ST WORLD

3RD WORLD

Activities

1. In your own words, explain how the debt crisis came about.
2. Did the money given in loans always reach the people it was intended for? Explain your answer.
3. Why don't governments of poor developing countries spend more on health and education?
4. Give two effects of world debt that can be seen in First World countries.
5. Name a group that called for the cancellation of Third World debt.
6. What point is Dominga de Velaques of Bolivia trying to make?
7. Name three other factors that block development in Third World countries.

4

Study 50 The Arms Trade

The United Nations Development Report estimates that to provide the people of all the developing countries with:

● basic education would cost $6 billion	(in the USA $8 billion is spent on cosmetics each year)
● water and sanitation would cost $9 billion	(in Europe €14 billion is spent on ice cream each year)
● basic healthcare would cost $15 billion	(in Europe €22 billion is spent on pet food each year)

Every day, on a worldwide scale, military spending amounts to approximately $2 billion. The five largest arms suppliers in the world are the USA, Russia, the UK, France and Germany.

Over seventy countries (mainly in the First World) manufacture light weapons and ammunition. The sale of small arms has caused approximately ninety per cent of recent war casualties; most of these casualties (ninety per cent) were civilians. There is no effective international code of conduct when it comes to selling weapons, which means that dictators and human rights abusers can still buy as many weapons as they can afford. In Angola, for example, it has been possible to buy an AK-47 for less than $15 or simply exchange one for a bag of maize. The vast majority of the twenty million refugees around the world (and the even greater number of internally displaced people*) are fleeing armed conflicts.

Global military spending amounts to over $800 billion each year

> * An internally displaced person is someone who has left his or her home in fear of persecution but has not crossed the border.

 Activities

Military Spending

1. According to the United Nations Development Report how much would it cost to provide basic education to all in developing countries?

2. Name three of the largest arms suppliers in the world.

3. Do you think there should be a code of conduct when it comes to the sale of arms?

4. Explain in your own words who an internally displaced person is.

East Timor

Arms supplied to countries with **unstable governments** or **military dictatorships** can have disastrous effects for the countries' citizens. An example of a country that has suffered greatly because of the arms trade and the economic interests of other nations is **East Timor**.

East Timor used to be a colony of Portugal. Ten days after gaining independence in December 1975, East Timor was invaded by troops from Indonesia, which was run by a dictator, President Suharto. Between 1975 and 1999 one-third of the population, about 250,000 people, died as a direct result of the invasion.

The USA supplied about ninety per cent of the weapons used in the invasion. The USA was keen to maintain good trading relations with Indonesia, which has resources such as timber and rubber. Australia did not condemn the Indonesian invasion because of oil reserves in the Timor Straits Sea. Australia lobbied the UN on behalf of Indonesia and was rewarded in 1989 when a treaty was signed which shared out East Timor's oil reserves between the two countries.

Britain also became a main supplier of weapons to Indonesia and their Hawk warplanes were used against villages in East Timor.

In 1996, in Britain four women spent six months in prison for using a hammer to damage a Hawk aircraft which was due to be delivered to Indonesia.

The case made legal history after the jury acquitted the four on the grounds that they were justified in trying to prevent an act of genocide. ➡

An Australian peacekeeper in East Timor

Despite many **United Nations resolutions** condemning the invasion of East Timor as an illegal act, Indonesia continued to occupy East Timor. Finally, due to international pressure a referendum of the people was held in August 1999, when the majority voted for independence. The Indonesian army and local militia refused to accept this decision, and in the violence that followed, seventy-five per cent of the population was internally displaced or forced to move to Indonesia. It is almost impossible to say how many were murdered.

During the period of terrible violence, the EU put a ban on arms exports to Indonesia but lifted it four months later. The Indonesian arms market is worth millions of euros to EU arms manufacturers.

After the vote for independence a United Nations peacekeeping mission moved into East Timor and helped restore order. In August 2001 the people of East Timor took part in the **first ever democratic elections**.

In May 2002 the East Timorese people celebrated their independence. Kofi Annan, General Secretary of the UN, was present at the celebrations and stood with the new president of East Timor, Gusmao. The UN blue flag was lowered by a UN soldier to the tune of **'We Shall Overcome'**. Then the black, red and white East Timor flag was raised while the new national anthem of East Timor was sung.

A young East Timorese waving the country's new flag

However, human rights problems still exist, especially in Indonesian West Timor, where approximately 60,000 East Timorese refugees remain.

East Timor and Ireland

The **East Timor Ireland Solidarity Campaign** was founded in Dublin in 1992 after a group of unemployed people in Ballyfermot saw a documentary on the situation in East Timor. They were shocked and angered by what they saw and decided to start up the East Timor Ireland Solidarity Campaign. The campaign was run from the house of Tom Hyland in the early years. Since then it has become one of the best respected human rights campaigns in the world. Tom Hyland was awarded a People of the Year award for his work on East Timor and now lives there.

Through CSPE classes a number of secondary school students became involved in a project with Oran Doyle of the East Timor Ireland Solidarity Campaign. The project linked Irish

rights and responsibilities

schools with schools in East Timor. Students from both countries learned about each other through letters and photos that were exchanged. An exhibition of photographs that Irish students had sent toured the schools in East Timor. This school-links project has been shown on Timorese television, and in those areas where TV is not available it has been shown on the mobile television unit run by the UN.

 Activities

East Timor

1. Name the country that invaded East Timor.
2. What has the direct result of the invasion been?
3. Why did the USA supply ninety per cent of the arms for the invasion?
4. Why didn't Australia condemn the invasion?
5. Explain why a judge released four English women even though they had damaged a Hawk aircraft.
6. Do you see any conflict of interests between human rights and supplying arms to countries which may use those arms to terrorise or repress their citizens?

Study 51 Refugees

Over the past decade the number of **refugees*** has almost doubled. More than twenty million people worldwide have been forced to flee violence or persecution in their own country. **Almost eighty per cent of refugees are women and children**. People become refugees because of war, conflict, lack of democracy and human rights abuses.

Most of the world's refugees – ninety per cent – live in the developing world. Europe receives only five per cent of the world's refugees.

Under government-sponsored schemes, as part of a response to a particular crisis Ireland has accepted programme refugees**. Examples of these are: 212 Vietnamese refugees in 1979, 178 Bosnians in 1992 and 1,031 Kosovars in 1999.

🦾 Activities

1. What do you understand the term 'refugee' to mean?
2. Name two countries that Ireland has accepted 'programme refugees' from.
3. What do you understand the term 'asylum seeker' to mean?
4. Approximately eighty-five per cent of those who apply for asylum status in Ireland are refused. Are you surprised by this figure? Explain your answer.

The following newspaper article tells the story of how two young refugees came to be in Ireland and what their fears and hopes are.

The real question is – can we stay?

Imagine that you're just eighteen, alone and friendless in an alien country. Your family is dead – you witnessed their murders two years ago, but managed to escape abroad. Living alone in a tiny bedsit, you're struggling to put your life in order. You're attending a local school and in a few weeks' time you're to sit major exams.

Asylum seekers

You're trying to study, but are never quite sure whether you will be able to sit the exams after all. Your application for refugee status may be turned down any day now and you'll be forced to move on. You've already been refused asylum once and your case is on appeal. You don't dare believe that you will be allowed to stay. What will you do? Where in the world will you go? You've no one to turn to for help.

> *A refugee is someone who 'owing to a well-founded fear of being persecuted for reasons of race, religion, nationality, membership of a particular social group or political opinion, is outside the country of nationality and is unable, or owing to such fear, is unwilling to avail of the protection of that country'. (Geneva Convention 1951)

> **A programme refugee is a person who has been invited to Ireland because of a government decision which was made in response to requests from bodies such as the UNHCR.

human dignity

Landu and Robert in the offices of the Irish Refugee Council

'On the fifteenth of March, 1997 rebels came to my home,' says eighteen-year-old Landu Kulabutulu, who comes from the Democratic Republic of Congo, formerly Zaire. 'They burst open the door and murdered my parents and raped my sister. I escaped through the window and ran to the church. The priest helped me to escape from the country.'

Landu is now an **asylum seeker*** in Ireland. At home, he was studying to be a motor mechanic, but here he's attending school and working for his Junior Cert. exams. His mother tongue is Lingala – he knows only one other person who speaks the dialect in Ireland – and his second language is French. His English, he admits, is poor. 'I understand English and I'm getting better at speaking it – my teacher says I'm improving,' he says.

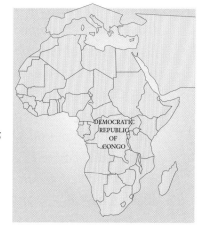

Last year Landu suffered a racist attack. He was beaten up by a gang and had to have sixteen stitches in his head. Nonetheless, he firmly believes that there are 'many good people in Ireland'.

If Landu is granted **refugee status****, he would like to go to English classes for six months and then go to college to train to be a mechanic. Meanwhile, he is struggling with his Junior Cert. Does he study? 'How can I study?' he asks. 'I've too much to think about. I have too many problems.

*An asylum seeker is a person who formally requests to live in another state because he/she has a 'well founded fear of persecution in their country of origin'. If their application is approved they can work or avail of social welfare benefits like an Irish citizen.

**Refugee status means that a person is entitled to live, work, receive health, education and other services on the same basis as an Irish citizen.

4

I've lost my parents. I don't think my life is worth living . . .'

We're sitting in the offices of the Irish Refugee Council. Alongside us is Robert, an eighteen-year-old Liberian, he's poring over a physics textbook. He nods at Landu's outburst. 'We need to know our lives are going to be all right,' he says. 'If I can't stay in Ireland, I don't know where I can go.'

Robert witnessed his father's murder when he was nine. Parentless, he tagged on to a group of people who travelled to Ghana to escape civil strife in Liberia. Two years ago, he stowed away on a ship and ended up in Ireland.

Like Landu, he finds getting down to study difficult. He, too, lives alone in a bedsit. 'I'm trying to study and work from 8 pm to midnight most nights. But after school, I have to go shopping, cook and eat and do my homework. It takes a lot of time.' He's clearly envious of the youngsters who have their meals handed up to them. Without all the other pressures in his life, he'd be enjoying the study, he says. His constant frustration, though, is the thought that it's just a waste of time and that by the start of the exams, he'll be – God knows where.

Children in a refugee camp

According to the Refugee Council, there are thirty-two separated children – unaccompanied minors who are seeking asylum – in Ireland. They come from a range of countries including a number of African states, Kosovo and Romania. The youngest is thirteen years old.

'The children come from zones of extreme conflict,' notes Sarah MacNeice, who is assistant co-ordinator at the Irish Refugee Council's legal unit. 'Many have lost their parents. The biggest problem facing this group of children is that they are completely alone', she says.

Many of the people who are forced to seek asylum abroad spend their time wishing they were back at home with the families and friends they've left behind. These separated children, however, have no family or friends at home. Ireland is all they've got.

(Taken from The Irish Times)

interdependence

Approximately ninety-two per cent of people who apply for asylum in Ireland are refused it. They can appeal against this decision. Of those that appeal, approximately eighty-five per cent **are not** granted refugee status.

 Activities

The real question is – can we stay?

1. Why did Landu leave the Democratic Republic of Congo?
2. Do you think it would be upsetting to live in a country where only one other person spoke your dialect? Explain your answer.
3. Why do you think it is difficult for Landu and Robert to study?
4. What do you think people should do for refugees who arrive in a country?
5. What do you think governments should do for refugees who arrive in a country?
6. What message do you think this poster is trying to get across? Give reasons for your answer.

ACTION

Questionnaire: Design a questionnaire that you could carry out with another class to see how much they know about the issue of refugees in Ireland. (Example of questionnaire on p. 208.)

Interview: Contact an organisation that is concerned with refugees and invite them to speak to the class.

Charter: Draw up a list of rights that you think asylum seekers should be entitled to.

SPOT THE REFUGEE

There he is. Fourth row, second from the left. The one with the moustache. Obvious really.

Maybe not. The unsavory-looking character you're looking at is more likely to be your average neighborhood slob with a grubby vest and a weekend's stubble on his chin.

And the real refugee could just as easily be the clean-cut fellow on his left.

You see, refugees are just like you and me.

Except for one thing. They have been forced to leave their country because of persecution or war. Everything they once had has been left behind. Home, family, possessions, all gone. They have nothing.

And nothing is all they'll ever have unless we extend a helping hand.

We know you can't give them back the things that others have taken away.

But we are asking you to keep an open mind. And a smile of welcome. It may not seem like much. But to a refugee it can mean everything.

UNHCR is a strictly humanitarian organization funded by voluntary contributions. Today, we are helping more than 22 million refugees around the world.

UNHCR
United Nations High Commissioner for Refugees

4

Discussion/Essay: If governments ensured the protection of human rights there would be no refugees. 'Human rights have no borders' (Amnesty International). Explain what you think is meant by this statement.

Study 52 Know Racism

In 2001 the **National Anti-Racism Awareness Programme** was introduced by the government. The Programme was set up because of concerns about reports of racist attacks and behaviour in Ireland and Europe. Racism is also an issue of concern for the EU and the UN.

Anti-Racism
is a key principle of community development

Good community development practice tackles the exclusion, discrimination and racism experienced by people on the grounds that they are Black, Travellers or members of other ethnic minorities, refugees or asylum seekers.

What is Racism?

- **Racism** is a form of discrimination (see p. 12) faced by **ethnic minority groups.***
- **Racism** is based on the false belief that some 'races' are superior to others.
- **Racism** denies people basic human rights, dignity and respect.

There are now 160 different nationalities living in Ireland. Ireland has undergone many changes in recent years. Our society is now a multicultural society. Irish people have always been known for their generosity and their friendly and welcoming spirit. Fear of strangers or lack of understanding of others could spoil this spirit.

What is Racist Behaviour?

Racist behaviour can take many forms. For example:

- leaving a person out or snubbing them because of their race, colour, national or ethnic origins
- making jokes or hurtful remarks or insults about a person
- physically hurting or threatening a person.

The Know Racism campaign looks at what can be done about racism.

> * An ethnic minority group is a group of people whose skin colour, religion or culture is different from the majority of people living in the same place.

What Can You Do About Racism? A Ten-Point Code To Follow

- Treat people from minority groups with the same respect you show to other people.
- Challenge, where appropriate, racist remarks and insults.
- Report racist incidents to the gardaí.
- If you see racial harassment occurring in a public place, such as a shop, cinema, restaurant, etc., inform the management.
- Support initiatives which help combat racism, e.g. wear the Know Racism emblem.
- Look for opportunities to establish and strengthen your personal ties with local ethnic, religious and cultural minorities.
- Extend a hand of friendship to persons of different cultural backgrounds.
- Do not prejudge or label people because of their cultural or ethnic origin.
- Teach children to respect different cultures.
- Make your workplace a comfortable environment for workers regardless of their ethnic or cultural background.
- We all have a responsibility to tackle racism.

What is an 'Intercultural Society'?

Ireland now has the opportunity to build a society that recognises that diversity and difference provide opportunities and benefits for all people who live here. An **intercultural** society is one which has a good interaction and understanding between different cultures.

Activities

1. What does racism mean?
2. Describe different forms of racist behaviour.
3. List five things you could do about racism.
4. What does an 'intercultural society' mean?
5. What do you think are the benefits of an intercultural society?
6. What could you do to help build an intercultural Ireland?

Study 53 Fair Trade and Ethical Trade

One way of creating a more equal world, protecting the rights of everyone and protecting the resources of the planet is to encourage fair trade. As consumers we often don't think about where many of the products we use are made or produced, or the working conditions and pay of those who make them.

Working for less than a bar of chocolate

Ricardo da Silva is a twelve-year-old boy who lives with his family on a large cocoa plantation in Bahia, Brazil. All nine people in his family work on the plantation collecting the cocoa beans which are used for making chocolate by large **multinational companies*** *such as Mars, Cadbury and Nestlé in their factories in Europe and North America. During the harvesting season, Ricardo's family picks the pods from the trees. Working in pairs, one person splits the pod with a machete while the other scoops out the beans.*

Even though Ricardo has worked with cocoa beans all his life he has never actually tasted chocolate. Even if he wanted to he couldn't afford to buy it. He earns less than 38 cent a day. On a number of occasions people have lost their jobs on the plantation when the amount of Brazilian cocoa beans needed by the large chocolate companies fell. The plantation owner didn't want to lose money so he fired some of the workers. Sometimes the price of cocoa beans has dropped on the world market. When this happens, Ricardo and his family are paid even less by the plantation owner.

Cocoa beans drying on a plantation

Ricardo is not the only one in this situation: there are three million children working as hard and earning as little as Ricardo in Brazil today.

Activities

Ricardo's Story

1. Name three multinational companies in Ricardo's story.
2. Why hasn't Ricardo tasted chocolate?
3. What happens to the plantation workers when less cocoa beans are needed by large chocolate companies?

* Multinational companies are companies with operations in more than one country around the world. They are also sometimes referred to as transnational companies (TNCs).

Fair Trade

As we have seen, we rely on basic food commodities such as coffee, tea, sugar and cocoa. Many of these natural products are grown in Third World countries. For example, over forty Third World countries grow coffee and most of the world's coffee beans are grown on small family plots of less than two acres. Coffee is the world's second most important commodity (oil being the first). The people who grow these products often work for low wages and in bad working conditions.

Fair Trade means that people receive fair wages for their products and enjoy decent working conditions. If the peoples of the developing world were treated fairly by the multinationals, they would have more money to spend on basics like health, education and housing.

The **Irish Fair Trade Network** aims to increase the sale of fair trade products in Ireland and so allow people in developing countries to earn a living with **dignity**. Examples of fair trade products are Café Direct, Bewleys Direct and Robert Roberts coffee. This coffee is sold in many large supermarkets throughout Ireland. When you buy a fair trade product

Young people protesting for Fair Trade

you can be sure that the growers have received a guaranteed fair price for their product and have better control over working conditions. Without fair trade, coffee producers would receive only eight per cent of the final price of a jar of coffee.

Many Oxfam shops throughout the country also sell fair trade products like textiles, tea and crafts.

 Activities

Fair Trade

1. Explain what you understand 'fair trade' to mean.
2. In what ways would fair trade improve the lives of people in the developing world?
3. What does the Fair Trade Network do?
4. Give an example of a fair trade product.

Ethical Trade

While fair trade is mostly concerned with ensuring a fair deal to small producers in the developing world, ethical trade refers to

Barbie

companies that aim to meet minimum standards in the production of their goods. These standards can relate to protecting the workers or protecting the environment.

Young workers making Nike products in a factory in South China

Behind many brands are large **multinational companies**. Multinational companies now control over seventy per cent of world trade. While they provide jobs and much-needed investment in the Third World, irresponsible practices can cause more harm than good. For example, multinational companies can move the production of their goods to countries with the lowest wages, lowest taxes or lowest standards of care for the workers and then return the profits to the home country.

For example, if a Barbie doll is selling in the USA for $9.99:

- ⊕ $7.99 will go on transport, retailing and profit in the USA.
- ⊕ $1 will be shared by transporters and agents in Hong Kong.
- ⊕ 65 cents will be spent on raw materials.
- ⊕ The remaining 65 cents will be spent in the country of manufacture (China).
- ⊕ Workers' wages are a small fraction of the 65 cents. *(AMRC 1998)*

Many companies are becoming more powerful than governments. The Shell company, for example, has annual sales three times the income of Nigeria. Such companies have the power to make or break communities.

The Shell company has been much criticised by environmental and human rights groups for its operations in Nigeria, where the lands of local communities (such as those of the Ogoni tribe) have been polluted.

Multinational companies that depend on the First World to buy their products do respond to pressure. For example, Del Monte responded to a '**One World Development**' campaign by agreeing to recognise independent trades unions on its banana plantations in Costa Rica. Workers are now able to negotiate for better conditions without fear of losing their jobs.

Action in this case worked. Here is what one worker has said.

'It might seem like a trivial thing to send off postcards to Del Monte, but it's not trivial to us. You have actually forced the multinational to meet us and discuss face to face, something which has not happened for many years.'

(Carlos Arguedas is a banana worker in Costa Rica and a member of the trade union SITRAP)

Do you think about where the food you buy comes from?

4

 Activities

Ethical Trade

1. What does 'ethical trade' mean?
2. Who has criticised the Shell Company for their operations in Nigeria?
3. What form of protest did the One World Development campaign take to help Del Monte workers in Costa Rica?

ACTION

Survey: Conduct a survey in your area to find out what type of coffee people drink and how much of it they drink. Find out if they know about fair trade coffee and whether or not they'd buy it.

Poster: Design a poster/leaflet to raise awareness about fair or ethical trade. Write to any organisation that is concerned with the developing world, like the Irish Trade Fair Network, the Irish Congress of Trade Unions and Trócaire, to find out more information that you could include in the poster/leaflet.

Study 54 Non-Government Organisations

Many Irish voluntary organisations or **non-government organisations** (NGOs), such as Trócaire, Concern Worldwide and the Irish Red Cross, provide aid to the people of the developing world. These organisations work in partnership with the people of these countries and money is used to provide such things as clean water supplies, health care and education.

Read **one** of the following case studies to find out about the kind of work these organisations are involved in.

Case Study 1 – Trócaire

Trócaire is the official overseas development agency of the Catholic Church in Ireland. Trócaire works to support long-term development projects overseas and to provide relief during emergencies and at home to inform the Irish public about the root causes of poverty and injustice. Trócaire means 'compassion' in the Irish language.

Claire O'Neill works for Trócaire as a project officer. She describes some of the work she is involved in.

What does being a project officer mean?
Trócaire project officers are responsible for the work of Trócaire in the developing world. In my case I am responsible

for programmes in Peru and Bolivia, two South American countries. The work of a project officer is to help Trócaire make decisions about the kind of programmes that best meet the needs of the poorer communities in Peru and Bolivia. In order to achieve this Trócaire works alongside local organisations.

Typical Trócaire-funded programmes are health care programmes for women and children, agricultural training for local farmers, day-care centres for street children and legal aid and legal defence for people who suffer human rights abuses.

Describe a project in which Trócaire is involved in Peru.

Trócaire is involved in a number of human rights projects throughout Peru. Peru has emerged from a very violent internal conflict between the guerrilla movement, the Shining Path, and the Peruvian military, which left over 30,000 dead and many communities displaced. Thousands of people still remain in prison, many unjustly accused of terrorism.

Trócaire supports the Institute for Legal Defence (IDL), an organisation that defends the rights of innocent people who have been unjustly imprisoned or tortured. It also educates people about their rights as citizens, how to defend themselves and how to ensure a fair trial. In many rural parts of Peru people live in such isolated areas that there is no local authority or government representation. Many rural people do not have the opportunity to get an education, therefore, human rights organisations such as IDL work with community leaders. They help them to understand their country's justice system and its laws in order to better defend themselves and participate as citizens of their country.

Among its many activities Trócaire runs a campaign every year during Lent to highlight a different issue of global concern, such as child slavery.

4

 Activities

Case Study 1

1. What region is Clare O'Neill of Trócaire responsible for?
2. What kind of programme does Trócaire fund in Peru?
3. Why is Trócaire involved in human rights projects in Peru?
4. What is the work of the Institute for Legal Defence in Peru?
5. How does having no local authority or government representation affect the lives of people living in rural Peru?
6. Do you think that the work agencies like Trócaire do is important? Explain your answer.
7. Name three other organisations that concern themselves with the developing world.

Case Study 2 – Concern Worldwide

Concern works in long-term development work, responds to emergency situations and undertakes development education. Read the following case study to see the kind of work Concern is involved with in Mozambique.

Mozambique's long-running conflict prevented many from receiving an education, but a successful Concern programme is helping them make up for lost time.

Schools in Mozambique cannot cope with the number of pupils who want to enter school. As a result, there are strict rules governing entry into the system. It is impossible for many to start school after the age of nine.

One of those who is currently at school as a result of the Concern programme is fourteen-year-old Quitera Joanquim.

'I was born in Zimbabwe when my parents were refugees there,' he explains. 'I went to school in Zimbabwe, but there we spoke Xhona and English, not Portuguese. I came back to Mozambique when I was ten. It was hard to learn the new language. Since then, my father has died and ➤

interdependence

my mother speaks only Xhona. I have seven brothers and seven sisters. Some of them are in this class too. I would like to become a teacher.'

But it is not only returning refugee children who benefit from this Concern programme. There are many other children who, for one reason or another, were unable to start school at the right age.

Children at school in Mozambique

Fransisco Inez is also fourteen years old. He started school at the age of ten and is repeating second year at the moment. 'I never went to school when I was younger. There was no money for it. I helped my father on the land, just like my six brothers and sisters. Then my mother died and it was even harder for us.

Concern has helped build wells

'Now my older brother has a small business. He pays for me and one of my brothers to go to school and learn to read and write. I like school, I like it a lot. When I grow up I want to be a good person. I don't know what job I will do, but I will work hard.'

The following programmes are central to Concern's work in Mozambique.

Emergency

- ⊕ Overall, 21,000 families (147,000 people) supplied with emergency relief.
- ⊕ Food, seeds, tools and permanent shelter materials to over 5,000 families.
- ⊕ Work on water and sanitation, malaria control, school and health clinic repair.
- ⊕ Roads and bridges repaired to ensure access.
- ⊕ Provision of shelter, water and sanitation in two camps for displaced people.

Education

- ⊕ Seventeen new classrooms built for 2,550 children.
- ⊕ 850 school desks supplied, electricity installed in two schools, six latrines and two wells built.

➔

4

- Over 6,000 children availed of a mobile library service.
- Exercise books and pens supplied to 1,950 students in a youth literacy scheme.
- Two women's literacy courses also supported.

Health
- Following a government request, 3,688 people vaccinated against a range of diseases and Vitamin A supplements given to 1,233 children.
- Nine wells built to service over 700 people with water.

Activities

1. Give two reasons why some children in Mozambique are not able to get an education.
2. What do you think the benefits of going to school are?
3. Why do you think it would be important to fix roads and bridges?
4. Why do you think the people of Mozambique have to pay to be educated?
5. Name some rights that you think the people of Mozambique are being denied.
6. Do you think that the work agencies like Concern Worldwide do is important? Give reasons for your answer.
7. Name three other organisations that concern themselves with the developing world.

One way Concern tries to raise awareness of the work it does is by holding the Concern Fast. Over 56,000 people participated in the Concern Fast 2000, raising over €1.27 million in the process. Participation in the fast was particularly high among second-level schools, with the pupils of Colaiste Bríde, Clondalkin, Co. Dublin collecting the astonishing sum of £14,450 (€18,350) – the highest raised by any school, north or south.

The Department of Foreign Affairs and the Role It Plays in Developing Countries

Besides advancing good relations with other countries around the world and promoting Irish culture abroad, **the Department of Foreign Affairs has special responsibility for overseas development assistance and human rights**. Through the Irish Aid programme it provides long-term and emergency support to developing countries.

development

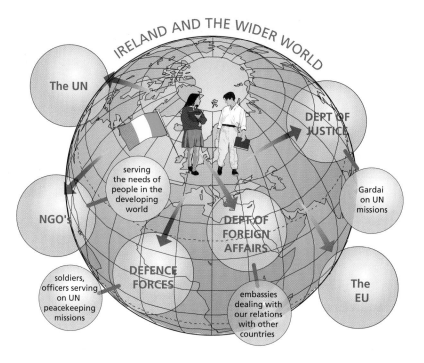

IRELAND AND THE WIDER WORLD

The UN

DEPT OF JUSTICE

serving the needs of people in the developing world

Gardai on UN missions

NGO'S

DEPT OF FOREIGN AFFAIRS

soldiers, officers serving on UN peacekeeping missions

DEFENCE FORCES

embassies dealing with our relations with other countries

The EU

Ireland Aid

The Irish government has an overseas aid and development programme. This programme is concerned with the basic needs and rights of the people of the developing world. **Ireland Aid** is the organisation that plans and delivers this programme.

Ireland Aid has helped fund the school these children attend in Nicaragua

Some of the ways Ireland Aid works are:

⊕ by working with the governments of countries in the developing world

⊕ by supporting the work of organisations like the UN and the development programme of the EU

⊕ by letting Irish citizens know about issues of concern in the developing world

⊕ by working with non-government organisations on specific projects in the developing world.

In 2000 Ireland Aid spent €210.3 million on various programmes. These programmes are about meeting basic needs like food, water, health and education. For example:

⊕ In Lesotho Ireland Aid, along with the Ministry of Natural Resource of Lesotho, provided clean drinking water to over 15,000 people.

4

In Zambia children speak many different languages. In all, eighty languages are used. For over thirty years English was the language used to teach all Zambian children. Ireland Aid supported a programme along with the government in Zambia which allowed children to work together in groups and learn to read and write in a local language.

Ireland Aid

Some of the other countries that Ireland Aid helps are Uganda, Mozambique, Ethiopia and Tanzania.

Activities

1. What is Ireland Aid?
2. How does Ireland Aid promote human rights?

Study 55 Ideas for Action Projects

Europe

1. Find out what countries have applied for EU membership. In groups, present a profile of each country in class.
2. Have a European day or week in school highlighting the culture, dance, food and traditions of other European countries.
3. Find out about the main ideas of the different political groupings in the European Parliament. Information can be obtained from the offices of the European Parliament at 43 Molesworth St, Dublin 2.
4. Interview a person who has lived in another EU State about their experiences of living, working or studying there.
5. Find out if your town is twinned with another town in Europe and, if so, how this happened.

Developing Our World

1. Contact an aid agency and find out about their work.
2. Design a poster or leaflet highlighting the work of an aid agency.
3. Hold a fundraising event for a cause you have found out about.
4. Find out where fair trade products are sold.
5. Design a poster highlighting fair trade or ethical trade.

human dignity

Remember to look back over the action ideas that are suggested throughout the chapter for more topics for an action project.

In chapter 5 you will find advice and helpful hints on how to do posters, leaflets, surveys, interviews, petitions and fundraising events.

In the assessment section of chapter 5 you will find a breakdown of exactly what kind of information is needed for all sections of a Report on an Action Project (RAP) and a Coursework Assessment Book (CWAB).

Study 56 Revision Questions
(Revised Exam Format – 80 Marks)

Section 1 – 18 Marks
Answer ALL questions.

1. Which **two** of the following politicians are Irish MEPs?   (4 marks)
    (i)   Brian Crowley   ❒
    (ii) Tony Blair   ❒
    (iii) Patricia McKenna   ❒
    (iv) Liz O'Donnell   ❒

2. Indicate whether the following statements are **True** or **False** by placing a tick beside the correct answer.   (4 marks)

		True	False
(a)	Ireland has twenty-one MEPs.	❒	❒
(b)	The Treaty of Rome set up the European Economic Community.	❒	❒
(c)	Irish MEPs sit together as a national group in the European Parliament.	❒	❒
(d)	Many people die in the Third World from preventable diseases.	❒	❒

3. Match each letter in column X with the number of its corresponding pair in column Y.

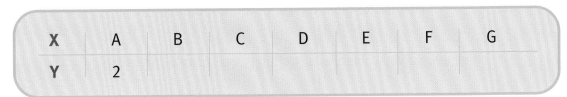

X	A	B	C	D	E	F	G
Y	2						

X

A. The European Commission
B. Developing countries
C. The European Court of Justice
D. The Council of the European Union
E. An NGO is
F. The European Parliament
G. Jubilee 2000 is

Y

1. has the final say on what becomes EU law.
2. suggests/proposes new laws.
3. debates suggestions/proposals for new laws.
4. decides if a national law that affects you contradicts an EU law.
5. a campaign to cancel Third World debt.
6. are sometimes called the South or Third World.
7. a voluntary organisation like Trócaire, Goal and Oxfam.

4. Fill in the missing words in the following sentences. (4 marks)

(a) In 1957 six European states signed the Treaty of _____, which set up the European Economic Community (EEC).

(b) In 1973, the UK, Denmark and _____ joined the EEC.

(c) Under the _____ Treaty, countries agreed to introduce a single currency by 1 January 1999.

(d) Under the _____ Treaty, it was agreed that the EU would become involved in peacekeeping and humanitarian missions.

interdependence

Section 2

Answer the THREE questions numbered 1, 2 and 3 below.
Each question carries 14 marks.

1. Read the letter and answer the questions that follow.

Dear Nick,

I am writing to let you know about the Irish Fair Trade Network Banana Campaign that we are running in our school.

We rang and asked a speaker from the Irish Fair Trade Network to come and give a talk to our class. She explained to us that bananas are the fifth most important item that is traded in the world, and that the EU is the largest importer of bananas in the world. Most of the bananas come from Latin American countries.

She also explained that these bananas are known as 'dollar' bananas. The 'dollar zone' refers to bananas grown on huge plantations owned by multinational companies where the workers are poorly paid. Nearly all of Ireland's bananas come from the 'dollar zone'. Small farmers who grow bananas make very little money because a lot of the profit goes to 'middlemen' and people who package and ship the bananas.

What do you think about that? Would you be interested in getting involved in our campaign to see that small banana producers get a better deal?

Love,

Ann

(a) What is the name of the campaign Ann is writing about?   (2)
(b) Who is the largest importer of bananas in the world?   (2)
(c) Where do these bananas come from?   (2)
(d) What is the 'dollar zone'?   (2)
(e) According to the letter above, why do the plantation workers themselves
     make so little money?   (2)

(f) If you as part of your CSPE class were to run a Fair Trade campaign in your school, describe two effective actions you could take.

Action 1   (2)

Action 2   (2)

2. Examine the headlines below and answer the questions that follow.

Access to cinema denied to wheelchair user

Romanians seek asylum after arriving by ship in Rosslare

Emergency accommodation not enough for growing number of homeless in our cities

Women and children leave villages in Sierra Leone as rebel groups attack

(a) Name three groups which you believe are being denied their rights either at home or abroad.

Group 1   (1)

Group 2   (1)

Group 3   (1)

(b) State what main right is being denied.

Group 1   (1)

Group 2   (1)

Group 3   (1)

(c) Take one group you have mentioned above and state which NGO or voluntary organisation is concerned with their plight.   (2)

(d) Describe what you know of the work of the organisation you have mentioned above.   (4)

(e) What day in the year is chosen/designated as International Human Rights Day? (2)

3. Examine the graph and answer the questions that follow.

(a) Using the graph, state which country has the highest turn-out of first-time voters.
                                                                                           (2)

(b) Which country has the lowest turn-out of voters?   (2)

(c) What must your name be listed on in order for you to vote?   (2)

(d) How old must you be to be eligible to vote in a European election?   (1)

(e) How often do elections for the European Parliament take place?   (1)

(f) There are many ways in which citizens of the EU can influence events in Europe.
     State a European issue that concerns you and state two actions that you could take
     to influence the European Parliament.

     European Issue   (2)

     Action 1   (2)

     Action 2   (2)

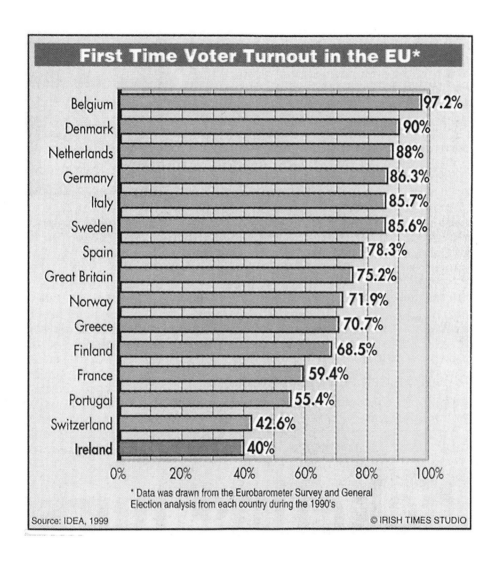

First Time Voter Turnout in the EU*

Country	Turnout
Belgium	97.2%
Denmark	90%
Netherlands	88%
Germany	86.3%
Italy	85.7%
Sweden	85.6%
Spain	78.3%
Great Britain	75.2%
Norway	71.9%
Greece	70.7%
Finland	68.5%
France	59.4%
Portugal	55.4%
Switzerland	42.6%
Ireland	40%

* Data was drawn from the Eurobarometer Survey and General
Election analysis from each country during the 1990's

Source: IDEA, 1999   © IRISH TIMES STUDIO

4

Section 3
Answer ONE of the questions numbered 1, 2 and 3 below.
Each question carries 20 marks.

1. Your CSPE class has decided to find out more about the UN and the part Ireland plays in UN peacekeeping missions.
    (a) Write a letter to an army representative outlining the purpose of such a visit.
    (b) Outline **three** questions you would like to ask and why you think they are important.
    (c) Describe how you would let the rest of the school community know about the role that Irish soldiers play as part of UN peacekeeping missions.

2. In an article for your school newsletter you are writing about major issues that young people in the Third World are/will be faced with in the 21st century.
    (a) Outline **three** major issues in your article that you have identified.
    (b) Describe or suggest **two** ideas that would highlight these problems more effectively.
    (c) Suggest what kind of photo/illustration or slogan would draw students' attention to such an article.

3. You have been invited to design an information leaflet to inform young people about Ireland and the EU.
    (a) Briefly outline the main EU institutions.
    (b) Explain how Ireland has benefited from membership of the EU.
    (c) Name and describe a major issue facing the EU.

 Now test yourself at **www.my-etest.com**

democracy

05 chapter

Assessment for CSPE

- Action projects and the skills you need
- Report on Action Projects (RAPs) and Coursework Assessment Books (CWABs)
- Revision for Junior Certificate Written Exam

Study 57 Action Projects and Skills

As part of your Civic, Social and Political Education course, you and your classmates will undertake an action project. You will see ideas for action projects throughout the book.

Read the **outline of Report on an Action Project (RAP)** and **Coursework Assessment Book (CWAB)** in Study 58 to get an idea of how to plan your action.

Your action can be as part of a group or on your own. It is where you become actively involved in developing a topic or an issue which interests you and that you wish to find out more about. By doing an action project you will develop new skills (e.g. information gathering and communication skills) and reinforce the new knowledge, skills and attitudes you have developed through your study of CSPE. In your action project you MUST reflect the **human rights and social responsibility** dimension of this course.

The action project MUST:

- have a link with one of the **seven CSPE concepts**
- involve a **genuine action**
- have an involvement with **people/community**
- have a **human rights and social responsibility** dimension.

The action could take the form of:

- **information posters**
- **surveys**
- **questionnaires**
- **student council activity**
- **designated day**
- **mock election**

- **inviting a guest speaker (interview)**
- **awareness week**
- **letter writing (information gathering)**
- **petitions**
- **information leaflets**
- **fundraising**
- **a visit**
- **wall display**
- **public speaking**
- **fact sheet / publication**
- **investigation**

Skills

By doing an action project you may develop new skills or improve the skills you already have.
Some new skills could be:

- discussing
- listening
- researching and gathering information
- selecting and sorting information
- analysing and evaluating (picking out important pieces of information and deciding why some information should or should not be part of the action)
- co-operating and working as part of a team or group
- planning and preparing for an interview or guest speaker
- designing and carrying out a survey/petition/questionnaire
- letter writing
- making phone calls or sending e-mails and faxes
- using the computer
- word processing
- negotiating with others
- planning, designing and presenting posters or wall displays
- debating issues and topics
- planning and organising a fundraising event
- presenting information or findings in a graph or chart
- holding a vote or election
- budgeting
- reporting
- running an awareness campaign.

It is important that while you are taking part in an action project that you keep a log or diary of the different activities you were involved in and what others did too. This will help you later when you have to write up your individual report on the action project.

The following information may help you when you are organising your action project.

Planning a Group Action

One way to plan an action is for the class to be divided into groups. Each group has responsibilities for certain jobs. It is helpful to keep a **diary** of the jobs you are involved in with your group; this will help you when you have to write your report later. Also **keep a note of the jobs the other groups in the class are doing** too so you can mention this in your report later.

The following is an example of the groups and the different responsibilities and jobs students could have if the class action involved inviting in a guest speaker.

The Liaising Group
- ⊕ ask principal for permission to invite guest speaker into the school
- ⊕ inform principal of the date and time the speaker will be in
- ⊕ ask permission to put announcement of visit in the day events/intercom notices
- ⊕ invite principal to the talk
- ⊕ invite other teachers and tutors to the talk.

development

The Questions Group

- brainstorm questions with all students
- select questions to be asked on the day
- prepare questions on cards
- nominate students to ask the different questions
- arrange back-up people in case of absences on the day.

The Recording Group

- organise how the answers to the questions will be recorded
- organise who will record what
- decide what will be done with the information gathered after the talk, e.g. summary to rest of class in next lesson
- suggest possible follow-up events or actions.

The Contact Group

- find name of organisation and person to contact for visit
- phone or write to speaker asking them to visit
- forward questions that will be asked
- greet speaker on arrival at school
- introduce speaker to the rest of the class
- thank speaker at end of interview/talk
- send thank-you letter from class to the speaker.

The Room-Organising Group

- arrange chairs in room for students
- arrange chair and table for speaker
- organise tea/coffee/water for speaker
- put room back in order after visit
- return any borrowed items like glasses, etc.

Plan for Action Project

Use this form to help you plan your action project.

What are we planning to do?

We want to find out more about environmental groups in our area.

205

5

We hope to find out about at least one group of environmentalists and what activities they do and what problems they are looking at.

What do we need to do?

- Find a directory or list of local groups from the local library.
- Contact each group and ask them to send us information and invite them to speak to the class.
- Arrange a suitable time to meet/talk to the speaker.

Who will we need to contact and why?

- The local librarian to get a directory of local groups.
- The local environmental groups for information and talks.
- Our teacher to pick a date for the speaker to come in.
- The principal to let them know when our visitor is coming.

What will we need to ask?

- How many members does your group have?
- Why did you join this group?
- What does the group do?
- Why do they do it?
- Where do you get the money?
- Are there ways that we could help?

stewardship

- We'll pass it on to the rest of the class and year group.
- We will decide with our classmates which organisation in the community might be able to help and how we might be able to help them, e.g. fundraising/designing a poster/information leaflets, etc.

Who in our group will do what and by when?

TASK	NAME	DEADLINE
Go to the library and get list of groups	Katie	Friday am
Arrange date for visits	Moya	Tuesday am
Write letters and send them	Eva	Thursday am

This plan can be used whether you are doing an individual action or a group action project. It would also be very useful for referring to when you start to write up your Report on an Action Project (RAP).

Remember to note what skills you used, e.g. drawing up a group plan = skills of organising, planning and working as part of a team; planning and writing a letter = skill of information gathering/research.

Keep an account of what you did if you worked as part of a group because you will need to state exactly what you were involved in as well as what your group did in your report, e.g. I made a phone call to an environmental group and asked them . . .

A good way to make a record of all you did is by keeping a diary of everything you do in and out of class.

Questionnaire

As part of an action project you may wish to find out information. One way to gather information is to use a questionnaire. Remember to plan what questions you wish to ask and to keep your questionnaire short so that it will not take people too long to fill out or for you to gather your findings. The following example of a questionnaire could help.

Note:
- the instructions given
- the different styles of questions
- the purpose of the questions.

5

QUESTIONNAIRE ON REFUGEES

Please tick the following:

1. **Sex:**   Male ☐   Female ☐

2. **Age:**   11–15 ☐   16–18 ☐   19–24 ☐
                    25–35 ☐   36–50 ☐   Over 50 ☐

3. **Most refugees are:**   Men ☐   Women ☐   Children ☐

4. **People become refugees mainly because:**
   They are fleeing persecution ☐   They are looking for work ☐
   They come here to learn English ☐   Other ☐

5. **Most refugees are in:**
   Europe ☐   Africa ☐   Asia ☐   America ☐

6. **What percentage of asylum seekers get refugee status in Ireland?**
   10% ☐   50% ☐   90% ☐

7. **Do you think the government is doing enough for refugees?**
   Yes ☐   No ☐   Don't know ☐

8. **Would you be happy if a refugee family came to live in your area?**
   Yes ☐   No ☐

9. **Do you think Irish people have responsibilities towards refugees?**
   Yes ☐   No ☐

10. **Do you think that all asylum seekers should be allowed to work while waiting for their case to be heard?**
    Yes ☐   No ☐   Don't know ☐

democracy

Survey

Carrying out a survey is another way of finding and gathering information.

Here are some points to note before you put your survey together.

- Decide on the questions you want to ask – use closed questions that require a yes/no answer, e.g. 'Do you know the name of the Taoiseach?' You could also ask questions that give a number of answers, e.g. 'How many TDs are in the Dáil?' a. 166 ☐ b. 110 ☐ c. 121 ☐
- Keep the survey short.
- Write out what your introduction will be, e.g. 'Hello. We are doing a survey about . . . would you answer some questions please?'
- In order to see if any changes are needed, practice your introduction and questions on your classmates beforehand.
- Decide on the number of people that you want to survey and photocopy that number of sheets.
- Decide when and where you will carry out the survey.
- Plan what you will do with the results of the survey, e.g. create a wall display, publish them in the school newsletter, etc.

The following example of a survey could help you to put your own together.

BULLYING SURVEY

Please tick the following:

1. **Which sex are you?**
   Male ☐   Female ☐

2. **Have you ever been bullied?**
   Yes ☐   No ☐

3. **Have you ever witnessed anyone being bullied?**
   Yes ☐   No ☐

4. **Which sex was the bully (bullies)?**
   Girl ☐   Boy ☐   Both ☐   →

5

5. **At what age were you bullied?**

    5–11 ☐   11–14 ☐   over 14 ☐

6. **When was the last time you were bullied?**

    Today ☐   In the last week ☐   Within the last month ☐

    Within the last 6 months ☐   A year or more ☐

7. **How often were you bullied?**

    Once ☐   Several times ☐   Almost every day ☐

    Several times a day ☐

8. **Where were you bullied?**

    Going to or from school ☐   In the school yard ☐

    At lunch time ☐   In the toilets ☐

    In the classroom ☐   In the changing rooms ☐

9. **If you were bullied, what sort of the bullying was it?**

    Physical ☐   Verbal ☐   Other ☐

10. **Do you consider bullying to be:**

    No problem ☐   Worrying ☐   Frightening ☐

11. **If you were bullied what effects did it have?**

    No effects ☐   Some bad effects ☐   Terrible effects ☐

12. **Who do you think is responsible when bullying continues to go on?**

    The bully ☐   The bully's parents ☐   Teachers ☐   The victim ☐

    The principal ☐   Students who witness the bullying but do nothing ☐

Petition

As part of an action project you may decide to organise a petition. A petition is used to raise awareness or to get support for a particular issue. Here are some points to note before you do your petition.

- ⊕ Use a clipboard so that people have something to write on.
- ⊕ State clearly what the petition is about at the top of the sheet.
- ⊕ Make sure you can explain the issue clearly if asked.
- ⊕ Decide when and where you will get the petition signed.
- ⊕ Prepare what you will say to people when you are asking them to sign the petition.
- ⊕ Be polite and thank people for their time.
- ⊕ Make sure the petition is sent to the people in a position to do something about the issue, e.g. local councillors, TDs, MEPs.

law

HELP US TO KEEP OUR STREETS CLEAN

We who have signed below ask the Council to provide more litter bins in our area.

NAME   ADDRESS   SIGNATURE

_____

_____

_____

_____

_____

_____

1 November 2002

To Councillor J. McCrea

Monaghan County Council

Co. Monaghan

We ask you to take into consideration the views of the people who have signed the enclosed petition.

Thanking you,

Jessica Kerins

Letter Writing

Letter writing is a good way to find out information from an organisation. Note the following points before you set about writing your letter.

- try to find out the specific person in the organisation to whom you should address the letter (e.g. youth officer, information officer)
- date your letter
- ask clear questions about the information you want
- be polite and thank the person for their help
- enclose a stamped addressed envelope.

5

16 High Street
Dingle
Co. Kerry

7 May 2004

Youth Officer
Amnesty International
Fleet Street
Dublin 2

Dear Sir/Madam,

As part of my Civic, Social and Political Education course in school I am doing a project on human rights throughout the world. On behalf of my class I would be grateful if you could send me any information you may have on this subject and any Urgent Actions that you are involved in at present.

We are also interested in fundraising for Amnesty International. Would you please send me any information on fundraising campaigns that you are running at the moment?

I look forward to hearing from you in the near future and thank you for your help.

Yours faithfully,

Sam Langan

Sam Langan

PS A stamped addressed envelope is enclosed.

You could send the letter by e-mail to the organisation if you find out their e-mail address and have access to a computer.

Guest Speakers

Guest speakers are often a useful way of finding out more about an organisation's work, the specific work of an individual or answering queries you may have over an issue that interests you.

The following form may help you in preparing for your guest.

Who is coming to see you? (Know their full name.)

Who will meet and greet the visitor when they arrive?

human dignity

Will you offer refreshments? If so, who will get them, how much will they cost and who will get them ready?

What exactly are you hoping to find out from your visitor? Make a list of questions to ask and decide who asks what question. (Avoid questions with a yes/no answer.)

Decide how you will record the interview, e.g. tape recorder, note taking.

What will you say at the end and who will say it?

You will also need to:

- give the person you want to interview good notice by phone or letter
- give your name, reason for the interview and examples of the questions that they will be asked
- agree a date and time, as well as the length of the interview
- decide what will be done with your findings, e.g. design an information poster or leaflet, use the information to help in a fundraising event, write an article for the school magazine or local newspaper
- write a letter of thanks to your speaker
- get permission and inform your principal of the date the visitor will be in the school
- keep a copy of this plan, as it will be very useful when you are writing up your Report on an Action Report (RAP). Note exactly what you did so you can mention this in your report.

Using the Phone

Using the phone is often a quick way of contacting an organisation and finding out information. When you phone an organisation remember to:

- say who you are and why you are phoning
- be polite and thank the person for helping you
- write out what questions you want to ask before you phone
- write out the main points of the phone call and what follow-up action, if any, needs to happen.

The following form could be filled out when you contact a person or organisation. This could be very useful to have when you are writing up your Report on an Action Project (RAP).

Name of organisation or person:

_____

Address:

_____

Tel/Fax/E-mail:

_____

Website:

_____

What is the organisation concerned with?

_____

Is it an international, national or local organisation?

_____

Do they provide leaflets, posters and fact sheets?

_____

Are speakers available to visit schools?

_____

Does the organisation charge for the speaker or written information?

_____

Other questions you need to ask about the organisation:

_____

Information you've learned:

_____

Follow-up action:

_____

One of these sheets can be kept for each organisation or person you contact in order to find out about a particular issue or topic that interests you.

E-Mail

Many organisations and groups can be contacted using e-mail. When using e-mail remember:
- open Outlook Express
- click the New Mail button on the toolbar
- in the **To** box, type the e-mail address of the organisation or person you wish to contact (e.g. cspe@netcom.ie)

- in the **Subject** box, type a heading for your e-mail (e.g. 'Interview for CSPE')
- type the message in the main part of the window. Use the same guidelines here as you would when writing a letter (see p. 211)
- to check the spelling click the spelling button on the toolbar
- click the **Send** or the **Send/Recv** button on the toolbar.

Fact Finding

A list of organisations and websites that may be helpful are in the appendix to this book. You could also find more information from:

- libraries
- local community organisations
- local authority offices
- the Internet.

Posters

Posters can be used to advertise an event or highlight something you think is important. When planning a poster consider the following:

- decide what is the main message that you want to get across
- decide how you will do this – what sort of style, images, pictures and text will get your message across best
- use clear lettering
- do a rough copy and make sure the poster can be read from a distance, and check for errors
- decide where you will put the poster for maximum attention
- don't forget to take down the poster after the event or awareness week.

Leaflets

Leaflets are a useful way of informing people of an issue that concerns you. Consider the following points before you put your leaflet together.

- decide why you want to produce a leaflet, e.g. to make people more aware of an issue, to get support/donations for a cause or to get across specific facts on a topic
- decide what main points your leaflet should contain about the topic, issue or event

5

- decide if you will use pictures, diagrams or graphs in your leaflet design
- decide whom you will give the leaflets to and how this will be done
- decide how many photocopies are needed and how much this will cost.

Fundraising

Raising funds for an organisation or cause you have found out about could be part of your action. Consider the following points on fundraising:

- Contact the organisation you wish to raise money for and see if there are any events that they are organising. You could take part in that event. They could also give you ideas on types of events you could hold to raise money.
- Your fundraising event could take the form of a cake sale, a sponsored walk/run, a raffle, a sports event, a sponsored silence, etc.
- Choose a date, time and venue for the event.
- See if you can get free advertising for your event from your local radio station or newspaper.
- Check out whether you need special permission from anyone before the event can happen, e.g. school principal, local council or Garda Síochána. **Make sure that you are insured.** This is important for every event you may undertake.
- Organise sponsorship cards if needed and the collection of all the money when the event is over.
- Thank everyone who helped and let them know how much money was raised.

Study 58

Your Guide Through a RAP and CWAB

Through your Junior Certificate Exam in CSPE you will demonstrate your understanding of these seven key concepts.

- rights and responsibilities
- stewardship

- development
- democracy
- law
- human dignity
- interdependence.

CSPE is concerned with your being active citizens and it is through your action projects that you demonstrate how you can take action over an issue that concerns and interests you. This action project will form part of your results. When you write it up for your exam in a report or coursework book, you will be showing the knowledge, skills and attitudes you have developed while studying this course. The knowledge, skills and attitudes you have developed over the last three years are also examined in the written paper.

As you have seen, assessment in Civil, Social and Political Education will take the following form.
1. A written exam as part of your Junior Certificate 40%
2. A Report on an Action Project (RAP) 60%
   or
   A Coursework Assessment Book (CWAB) 60%

Once you have completed an action project the next step is to write up your findings. You write about your action project in either a Report on an Action Project (RAP) **or** a Coursework Assessment Book (CWAB). You can find out what is needed in the RAP and CWAB and how they differ in the following pages.

Report on Action Project (RAP)

Before you do the final RAP make sure that you:
- **Do a draft or practice RAP** first. This will help you figure out what information you want to include in each section. You could get a photocopy of the Department of Education RAP booklet that is used for the report and practice in it.
- Make sure you **go back over your diary or log** to remind yourself of all the activities and information you discovered and were involved in.
- Check that the **action project you did has all the elements** needed. (See p. xi of 'About CSPE'.)
- **Don't include any extra pages** or photocopies in the RAP booklet.
- You **don't have to fill in every line** of the RAP booklet.
- Remember every student in the class must write their **own individual report**.

- Sort out exactly what is being looked for on each page of the RAP. The following section will help you do that.

The following is a breakdown of how a RAP is marked and the kind of information the examiner is looking for in each section of your report.

Section		Maximum Mark Available
1	**Title**	3 marks
2	**Introduction**	
	(a) Identification and explanation of concept.	4 marks
	(b) One other reason.	4 marks
3	**Activities Undertaken**	
	(a) Type of action and communication with people.	4 marks
	(b) List and description of activities.	15 marks
	(c) Detailed account of one activity.	15 marks
	(d) Application of skills.	15 marks
4	**Summary of Information**	30 marks
5	**Reflections**	30 marks
	TOTAL	120 marks

Title (3 marks)

- The title should give a **clear idea of the action** that has been taken. You could also mention here the **skill** involved in the action, e.g. 'a questionnaire investigating the issue of discrimination against people with disabilities' or 'learning about democracy by running a mock election'.
- Remember also to **tick the box** beside the type(s) of action that was undertaken as part of the action project, e.g. visit, interview, etc.

Introduction (8 marks)
Part A (4 marks)

- Remember to **tick the box** beside the concept(s) your action project was based on, e.g. democracy, human dignity, etc.
- Explain how your action project was **based on this/these concepts**.

218

- Give **one reason** why you chose this action project.
- Give **a clear reason why** you did this particular action project. Avoid repeating what you said in part (a).
- Avoid such phrases as 'our teacher told us to . . .'

Activities Undertaken (49 marks)

Part A (4 marks)

- Remember to **tick the box** beside the people communicated with in the course of your action project, e.g. students in my class, family, etc.
- Explain **why these people were communicated with** and why they were involved in the action project.
- Your answer should say **why the people or organisations that became involved** in your action project were important or relevant to the subject/topic of your action project.

Part B (15 marks)

- Write a **list and brief description** of the main tasks/activities undertaken as part of the action project.
- **What we did** . . . Each student should list the different activities they did during the course of the action project. This list will be the same for all students if the project was a group action, e.g. survey, interviewing, letter writing, collecting information, working in teams, etc.
- Include about **six activities, writing two to three sentences** describing each one.
- In a group action all **the activities of each group** in the class are listed and described even if you weren't involved in every one.

Part C (15 marks)

- Give a detailed account of **ONE particular task/activity** from the list in part (b) that **YOU undertook** as part of the action project.
- **What I did** . . . You should write out in detail an account of **one task** or activity you did.
- **Don't** write a number of different tasks or activities that you were involved in.

Part D (15 marks)

- Describe how **YOU** applied at least **TWO SKILLS** when undertaking the activity described in part (c) above.
- Write about **four sentences** on how you applied/used **each skill**.
- The skills you described cannot relate to the project in general. They **MUST relate** to

what you learned doing the **task** or activity you described in part (c) of Section 3. For example, if you had described writing a letter in **part (c)**, then the skills described here would explain how you improved your typing and computer skills and your knowledge of how to lay out a letter.

Summary of Information (30 marks)

- Give **FIVE** pieces of information or **facts** that you found out about the subject of the action project.
- Six marks are given to each of the five relevant facts or pieces of information given.
- Do not include any personal opinion here.
- Sentences which begin with **I learned . . ., I discovered . . ., I found out . . .**, etc. are helpful here.
- All facts **MUST** relate to the concept/theme/topic/subject/unit of the action project.

Reflections (30 marks)

- Think back on your action project and the different experiences you had while doing it. Give your **OWN thoughts** on these and explain why **YOU** think this way.
- This is where you make a number of **statements. You must give reasons for three of these statements**. In your reason or explanation say why you think or believe the way you do about the subject of the project, e.g. 'I think that the action project that I took part in has helped me understand how democracy works and why voting is an important part of a democracy' or 'It is my opinion that voting in elections is a good thing, as it is one of the ways we take part in running our country. If you don't vote your voice isn't heard.'
- Phrases like the following could be useful here:
  I think . . . because . . .
  It's my opinion that . . . because . . .
  I feel that . . . because . . .
- You could mention here how what you have learned could impact on you in the future and you could make recommendations or suggestions for future actions, e.g.
  I recommend that . . . because . . .
  In the future it would be helpful if . . . because . . .
- It is important that the views you express reflect the **human rights and social responsibility** dimension of the CSPE course.
- You can also make statements here about the **learning process and skills** acquired in doing the action project.
- Remember that it is not necessary that your action project had a successful outcome – sometimes things don't turn out the way we planned!

Read the following outline of a Report on an Action Project (RAP). This could help you get a good overview of the kind of information that can be included when writing up your report.

Report on Action Project

The Title of My Action Project

'Raising Awareness of the Importance of Fair Trade in My School'

Please tick √ the type(s) of action that was undertaken as part of the action project.

- ☐ Survey/questionnaire
- ☐ Interview
- ☐ Awareness raising
- ☐ Publication
- ☐ Campaign
- ☐ Designated day
- ☐ Guest speaker
- ☐ Mock election/parliament
- ☐ Fundraising
- ☐ Investigation
- ☐ Student council activity
- ☐ Visit   (3 marks)

Introduction

(a) Please tick √ the concept(s) on which your action project was based.

- ☐ Democracy
- ☐ Rights and responsibilities
- ☐ Human dignity
- ☐ Interdependence
- ☐ Development
- ☐ Stewardship
- ☐ Law

Explain how your action project was based on this/these concepts.

My action project was based on these concepts because fair trade will help bring about development and dignity for the people of the Third World. Also, it is our responsibility to see that the rights of others are protected, as we should see ourselves as a global family all dependent on each other, or 'interdependent'. (4 marks)

(b) Give ONE reason why you chose to do this action project.

We chose to do this action project because in our CSPE class we were looking at reasons why the Third World was so poor. We realised that the world's trading arrangements made it easier for the First World to get richer at the expense of Third World nations and that a solution was to promote more fairly traded goods.

We decided to do what we could to promote the sale of fair trade goods in our homes, in our school and in our community. (4 marks)

Activities Undertaken

(a) Please tick √ the people communicated with in the course of your action project.

☐ Students in my class
☐ Other people in my school
☐ Person/people in the community
☐ Individuals/organisations involved in this issue
☐ Family

Explain why these people were communicated with and why they were involved in the action project.

We visited Oxfam to find information and to see their selection of fair trade goods. We went back another day and bought a lot of chocolate and other fair trade goods and sold it to the students in our school at lunchtime in the canteen. (4 marks)

(b) Write a list and brief description of the main tasks/activities undertaken as part of the action project.

We did a brainstorm on the board of all the possible actions that we could take and then divided into six groups to undertake the following tasks:

Group A: Arranged visit to Oxfam to see what fair trade goods were on sale and buy some of their chocolate.

Group B: Arranged survey to find out what other class groups knew about fair trade goods.

Group C: Wrote to most well-known supermarket chains to ask that more fair trade goods be stocked.

Group D: Arranged petition to be sent with the letters to the supermarket chains requesting that they stock more fair trade goods.

Group E: Made posters to go up around the school advertising fair trade goods sale on a certain day.

Group F: Requested use of school intercom to advertise cards from Oxfam and fair trade gifts and sold a selection of what was available in the canteen at lunchtime on designated day.

(15 marks)

(c) Give a detailed account of ONE particular task/activity from the list in part (b) that YOU undertook as part of the action project.

My main task was to get as many students as possible to sign our petition requesting Irish supermarkets to stock more fair trade goods. To prepare for this task I was responsible for making out the petition sheets. I had to clearly type out what the petition was about at the top of the sheet. It said, 'We who have signed below ask that you stock more fair trade products in your supermarkets.' Underneath that there was spaces marked out for the person's name, address and signature. At the very bottom the petition said, 'We ask you to take into consideration the views of the students who have signed the enclosed petition.' I printed out the sheet and I photocopied one for each of my classmates and arranged clip boards that would make it easier for students to sign. I stood outside the canteen at lunchtime on a day we had agreed with our year head and I collected 150 signatures.

(15 marks)

(d) Describe how YOU applied at least TWO SKILLS when undertaking the activity described in part (c) above.

Persuasion skills: I learned that the best way to persuade someone to sign a petition is to know the facts of your argument very well so that you can speak directly to someone without looking down at your page. I had written out a number of key points of information that explained what fair trade was all about and why it was so important and practised it many times with other classmates before I had to face the rest of the school in the canteen. I also learned that you are more likely to get a positive response to a request if you speak politely and try not to be too pushy.

5

Computer skills: I learned how to format the petition in Word on the computer. I learned how to use a table and clearly organise information on a page. I also found out how to save it on a floppy disk so that I could work on it on any computer in the computer room in school, as it was hard to always get the same PC at lunchtime.

(15 marks)

Summary of Information

Give FIVE pieces of information or facts that you discovered about the subject of the action project.

- If the people in developing countries are paid a proper price for their work and their goods, they will be able to afford better health care and education for themselves and their children.
- Fair trade is an international movement which ensures that producers in poor countries get a fair price for their goods so that they can live their lives in dignity.
- Oxfam's 'Make Trade Fair' campaign aims to change world trade rules so that trade can make a real difference to the fight against global poverty.
- If Africa, East Asia, South Asia and Latin America were each to increase their share of world exports by one per cent, this could lift 128 million people out of poverty. (Source: Oxfam Report 2002, 'Rigged Rules and Double Standards'.)
- Many of the products that we depend on like tea, coffee, bananas and cocoa beans (used in chocolate) are produced in poorer countries in the South or Third World.

(30 marks)

Reflections

Think back on your action project and the different experiences you had while doing it. Give your OWN thoughts on these and explain why YOU think this way.

I think that fair trade really is the answer to helping the people in developing countries have a better quality of life and stop the massive inequality between northern and southern countries. Doing this project made me not only aware of human rights abuses in a very real way, but also brought home what the idea or concept of interdependence is all about. We need to think about all the stuff we use and where it comes from and what kind of conditions the people who produce it live in. We discovered, for example, that a lot of the cocoa beans produced in the Ivory Coast in Africa involves slave labour. I think that we should be more careful about our choices when shopping. I was disappointed that some of the supermarkets that we wrote to didn't reply to our letters and I think that more pressure should be put on them. I really enjoyed doing the petition and I think it made me more confident about explaining important issues. I even persuaded my mum to buy fair trade tea and coffee at home.

(30 marks)

Coursework Assessment Book (CWAB)

Instead of a RAP you could complete a Coursework Assessment Book (CWAB).

A Coursework Assessment Book is:

- a report on ONE module of work
- a module is twelve to fifteen weeks of work and includes an action project
- the module of work can be done at any time over the three years of Junior Cycle
- a module can be about a concept, unit or theme of work explored
- the CWAB is divided into **five sections**.

The following is an example of a twelve-week module on Human Rights and Racism in Ireland that could be undertaken and then written up in the Coursework Assessment Book (CWAB).

Week 1 Looking at human rights and ranking the United Nations Human Rights cards in order of importance.	**Week 2** Using Pastor Niemöller's poem (p. 22) and debating if the names of the groups mentioned in the poem could be changed to include groups that are denied their rights today.	**Week 3** Taking part in a 'walking debate' to decide and reach a decision on what groups in Irish society get a raw deal or who have certain rights denied.
Week 4 Finding out what organisations in Ireland are concerned with the rights of refugees.	**Week 5** Tracking stories in the newspapers that are about refugees and asylum seekers and seeing how these stories are reported.	**Week 6** Discovering what international laws Ireland signed in relation to refugees.
Week 7 Using a mix-and-match exercise of stories and definitions to find out what different terms mean, such as refugee, asylum seeker, etc.	**Week 8** Taking part in a role-play or freeze frame about trying to enter another country with no official documents.	**Week 9** Viewing the 'Know Racism' campaign video in preparation for the action project on racism in Ireland.
Week 10 Brainstorming and reaching a decision on what action to take over the issue of racism in Ireland.	**Week 11** Organising into class groups to prepare for a guest speaker.	**Week 12** Visit of guest speaker from the Irish Refugee Council.

5

After the twelve-week module of work is done the CWAB can then be completed. (An example of a completed CWAB based on this module can be seen later in this study.) It would also be very helpful if you **keep a log or diary** of all the activities you were involved in during the module. This will help you when you are filling out your CWAB booklet.

Before you do the final CWAB make sure that you:

- **Do a draft or practice CWAB** first. This will help you figure out what information you need to include in each section. You could get a photocopy of the Department of Education CWAB booklet that is used for the module and practice in it.
- Make sure you **go back over your diary or log** to remind yourself of all the activities and information you discovered and were involved in.
- Check that the **action project you did has all the elements** needed. (See p. xi of 'About CSPE'.)
- **Don't include any extra pages** or photocopies in the CWAB booklet.
- You **don't have to fill in every line** of the CWAB booklet.
- Remember every student in the class must write their **own individual CWAB**.
- Sort out exactly what is being looked for on each page of the CWAB. The following section will help you do that.

The following is a breakdown of how a CWAB is marked and the kind of information the examiner is looking for in each section.

Section		Maximum Mark Available
1	Title	3 marks
2	What My Coursework Module Was About	7 marks
3	Things I Have Done	
	(a) One class	20 marks
	(b) A second class	20 marks
	(c) A third class	20 marks
4	An Account of My Action Project	30 marks
5	Something I Have to Say	20 marks
	TOTAL	120 marks

Title (3 marks)

⊕ The title clearly says what the module was about.

⊕ The title should be linked to one of the seven concepts, e.g. 'Democracy and how it works in Ireland'.

What My Module Was About (7 marks)

⊕ Give a clear outline or overview of the module.

⊕ It should contain at least five points.

Things I Have Done (60 marks)

⊕ Give an account of three different classes you did during the module.

⊕ Each account is marked out of twenty marks.

⊕ In each case the topic, the description, what you learned and what you found interesting must be different.

⊕ Avoid repeating yourself in this section as you will not get the marks.

⊕ When you are asked in section 3 (c) 'One important thing that I learned from this class is . . .', you can write down a fact or a skill that you have learned.

⊕ Do not mention the action project here.

An Account of my Action Project (30 marks)

⊕ The action project must relate to the module, e.g. if your module was on 'The Law and how it works in Ireland', your action project could be a visit to the District, Circuit or High Court.

⊕ The action project is compulsory.

⊕ In part 4 of this section, 'Two things that I have learned from doing this action project are . . .', you can write two pieces of knowledge/facts or skills that you learned in doing the action project.

⊕ Avoid repeating any of the same information you used when writing your account of the three classes in section 3, you will lose marks if you do.

Something I Have to Say (20 marks)

The issue you write about in this section must be clearly connected to the overall module of work, not just the action project.

Read the following outline of a Coursework Assessment Book (CWAB) based on the twelve-week module on human rights outlined earlier. This could help you get a good overview of the kind of information that can be included when writing up your module and action project.

Coursework Assessment Book

Title

'Human Rights and Racism in Ireland'   (3 marks)

What My Coursework Module Was About

We did a number of classes about the issues of human rights and responsibilities. We looked at the United Nations Declaration of Human Rights and the Convention on the Rights of the Child. We looked at different groups in Irish society that are sometimes left out or not treated equally, like people who are homeless, the Traveller community and refugees. We talked about stereotyping and discrimination, what they mean and how this might lead to racist behaviour. We focused on discovering how racist behaviour towards refugees is a denial of human rights

(7 marks)

Things I Have Done

An account of ONE CLASS I found particularly interesting from this coursework module.

(a) The main topic of this class was . . .

About human rights.

(b) This is a short DESCRIPTION of what took place during this class.

In this class we looked at all the articles in the UN Declaration of Human Rights. These were written out on cards. The class was divided into groups. Each group ranked them in order of importance.

(c) ONE important thing I LEARNED from this class is . . .

I learned that the UNDHR contains rights that all human beings are entitled to, like 'everyone is born free and equal' or that 'no one should be subjected to torture or slavery'.

(d) What made this class particularly INTERESTING for me was . . .

I found this class interesting because we had a lot of debate in our group trying to agree which was the most important right a person could have. It was a very lively class and interesting to hear other people's opinions.

(20 marks)

An account of a SECOND CLASS I found particularly interesting from this coursework module.

(a) The main topic of this class was . . .

Understanding the difference between terms/definitions like 'asylum seeker', 'displaced person', etc.

(b) This is a short DESCRIPTION of what took place during this class.

We did a mix-and-match exercise where we had to match a correct term with a description of a person's situation, e.g. 'Lita was moved from one part of Sierre Leone to another because of civil war', so the term matched with this would be 'displaced person'.

(c) ONE important thing I LEARNED from this class is . . .

People move around the world for different reasons – some to escape war, famine or persecution and others because they wish to make a better life for themselves and get a better job.

(d) What made this class particularly INTERESTING for me was . . .

I had never before considered the different situations people can find themselves in and then have to move. Now I am more aware of the reasons why people have to move to another country.

(20 marks)

An account of a THIRD CLASS I found particularly interesting from this coursework module.

(a) The main topic of this class was . . .

Refugees on the move – treating people fairly and with dignity.

(b) This is a short DESCRIPTION of what took place during this class.

We had role cards of people in different situations, such as 'You have no passport or official documents, you have no belongings with you as you fled your country in fear of your life'. Then you had to try and convince another classmate who acted as a customs official to let you into his country. His role card said to keep you out.

How difficult it is to convince people you are who you say you are if you can't show a passport or speak with someone in the same language as yours.

I think that you understand better if you try and really step into someone else's shoes. It made me think more about how I would feel if this happened in my life.

(20 marks)

An Account of My Action Project for this Coursework Module

The TITLE of the action project I/we did as part of this coursework module was . . .

'Investigating Racism in Ireland – An Interview with an Asylum Seeker.'

One reason I/we did this particular action project was . . .

We wanted to meet first-hand somebody who knew what the situation was like coming to Ireland and trying to get refugee status here. We wanted to have a discussion with someone who had experience of the kind of difficulties you could meet in another country far away from your home.

ONE ACTIVITY I/we took part in during this action project was . . .

I had to contact a refugee organisation and see if they had a speaker available to come to our school. I wrote a letter explaining who we were and why we wanted someone from their orgainsation to speak to us.

TWO things I have learned from doing this action project are . . .

1. There are about 20 million refugees in the world that have had to leave their home.
2. Eighty per cent of the world's refugees are women and children.

ONE skill I used while doing this action project.

Letter writing skill.

A description of how I used this skill in my action project.

When I found the address of the organisation I wanted to contact to invite a speaker in from, I then did the following things.

- Checked my English book to see how to lay out a formal letter correctly.
- I decided that the letter would look better if it was typed out on the school computer.
- I put my address on the top right-hand corner of the page and the address of the organisation on the left.
- I kept the letter short and to the point.
- I thanked the organisation for their help.
- I enclosed a stamped addressed envelope.
- I learned to save my work on a floppy disk.   (30 marks)

Something I Have to Say Having Completed this Coursework Module

One ISSUE I feel strongly about or found interesting from this course-work module is . . .

I think that we must look out for the rights of others.

I feel STRONGLY about or found this issue INTERESTING because . . .

I feel strongly about this because we studied a poem in class which made the point that if you do not look out for the rights of others, then who will then look after your rights? For rights to work we all have to be responsible for them. I think that we put labels on people and stereotype groups that we do not know anything about or have never met.

What I CAN DO ABOUT IT or what I THINK CAN BE DONE ABOUT IT.

I can try and make sure that I treat all people with equal respect. I also think that there should be more government campaigns like the 'Know Racism' one which helps you to understand and gives you ten points to stop racist behaviour in Ireland.

(20 marks)

Study 59 Revision for Written Exam

- At the end of each chapter there are revision questions. Make sure you use these questions as part of your revision for the written exam, as the same style of questioning is used.
- Revise using the activities questions throughout the book.
- Follow newspaper and news reports to keep yourself up-to-date on current affairs and national and international news.
- Use the 2002 Civic, Social and Political Education Junior Certificate paper (provided in this book) to help you in your revision for the written exam.

5

🕀 Visit the Impact! website for more information, links to other useful sites and exam papers.

🕀 The written exam is divided into three sections:
  ● Section 1 (18 Marks): answer **all** questions
  ● Section 2 (42 Marks): answer **three** of the four questions
  ● Section 3 (20 Marks): answer **one** of the four questions.

Junior Cert. CSPE Exam Paper 2002

AN ROINN OIDEACHAIS AGUS EOLAÍOCHTA

JUNIOR CERTIFICATE EXAMINATION, 2002

CIVIC, SOCIAL AND POLITICAL EDUCATION

FRIDAY 7 JUNE – AFTERNOON 2.00–3.30

INSTRUCTIONS

1. Answer **all questions** in Section 1
    Answer **any three questions** in Section 2
    Answer **any one question** in Section 3.

2. **Write your answers in the spaces provided.**

3. **Hand up this paper at the end of the examination.**

<u>IMPORTANT</u>: **When you are answering the questions on this paper, you are expected to answer from the human rights approach of the CSPE course.**

Section 1
Answer ALL questions in this section.

1. The following photographs show people who hold, or have held, one of the four titles listed below. Put the correct title opposite each person shown in the photograph. You may use each title only **ONCE**.

Titles: Taoiseach
           Tánaiste
           Garda Commissioner
           Minister for Agriculture in the Northern Ireland Assembly

(a)_____

(b)_____

(c)_____

(d)_____

5

2. (a) For what do the initials of these **TWO** international organisations stand? You must complete each set of initials.

UN = U _____ N _____

EU =E _____ U _____

(b) For what do the initials of these two important human rights documents stand? You must complete each set of the initials. The initials H and R have already been completed.

UDHR = U _____ D _____ of Human Rights.

ECHR = E _____ C _____ of Human Rights.

(c) What are the correct initials given to the system of voting used in an Irish general election?
Tick √ **ONE** box only.

SV ☐

PR ☐

VT ☐

(d) Which important political figure lives in Áras an Uachteráin?

_____

(e) What are the names of the **TWO** houses of the Oireachtas?

_____ Eireann and _____ Eireann

(f) Explain the term 'by-election'.

_____

_____

(g) What government department is responsible for:
The Junior Certificate Examinations?

_____

The Defence Forces?

_____

(h) Which Irish court provides a service that investigates industrial disputes between trades unions and employers?

_____

(i) What is the name given to a local authority that is in charge of a county?

_____

3. Below is a list of **FIVE** organisations that are part of the European Union. The function of each of these organisations is described in the box below.

   Match each organisation with the description of its function by placing the letter indicating its function in the box next to it. One has already been completed as an example for you. You now have only **FOUR** to complete.

Organisation	Letter describing its function
The European Parliament	☐
The Council of Ministers	☐
The European Central Bank	b
The European Commission	☐
The Court of Justice	☐

FUNCTIONS OF THE ORGANISATIONS

(a) The organisation that brings together representatives directly elected by the people of each of the European Union member states.

(b) The organisation that looks after the financial and money affairs of the European Union.

(c) The organisation that decides whether individuals, groups or governments of the European Union have broken European Law.

(d) The organisation that brings together government ministers from each of the European Union member states to discuss the overall aims and direction of the Union.

(e) The organisation that draws up proposals for laws that are later passed by the Council and the Parliament.

Section 2
Answer any THREE of the questions numbered 1, 2, 3, 4 below.

1. **The Euro Changeover Board of Ireland**

   The following passage describes the work of the Euro Changeover Board of Ireland. Study it carefully and answer the questions that follow.

   Euro Changeover Board of Ireland

   On 1 January 1999, eleven Member States of the European Union formed the Economic and Monetary Union (EMU) and created a single currency, the euro, which came into being in cashless form on that date. On 1 January 2002, euro notes and coins were introduced into circulation, and Irish notes and coins began to be withdrawn.

   The Euro Changeover Board of Ireland was set up to carry out two basic tasks:
   ☐ to oversee the changeover to the euro
   ☐ to provide information.

   (a) What were the **TWO** basic tasks of the Euro Changeover Board?

   Task 1 _____

   Task 2 _____

   (b) EMU created the single currency, the euro. What does a single currency mean?

(c) Which **THREE** member states of the European Union have not joined the euro?

Country 1 _____

Country 2 _____

Country 3 _____

(d) State **TWO** reasons why joining the euro is good for Ireland.

Reason 1 _____

_____

Reason 2 _____

_____

(e) Describe **ONE** disadvantage for Ireland of joining the euro.

Disadvantage _____

_____

(f) Some people argue that we are giving too much political control to the EU and that this will not be good for Ireland. Do you agree with this statement? Please tick √ yes or no.

YES ☐   NO ☐

Explain you answer.

_____

_____

_____

2. **The Constitution of Ireland (Bunreacht na hÉireann)**

The following passage is taken from the Constitution of Ireland (Bunreacht na hÉireann). Study it carefully and answer the questions that follow.

'The State guarantees in its laws to respect, and as far as possible, by its laws to defend ... the personal rights of the citizen.

The State shall, in particular, by its laws protect ... the life, person, good name, and property rights of every citizen ...

The State guarantees liberty for the exercise of the following rights ... the right of the citizens to express freely their convictions and opinions ... the right of the citizens to assemble peaceably and without arms ... the right of the citizens to form associations and unions.'

(a) Name **TWO** rights that are mentioned in the passage in the box above.

(i) _____

(ii) _____

(b) What is the meaning of the following words as they are used in the passage in the box above?

The State _____

Liberty _____

Convictions _____

Associations _____

(c) When the right of the citizens 'to assemble peaceably' is mentioned in the Constitution, can you explain why the phrase 'without arms' has been included?

_____

(d)   The Constitution of Ireland can be changed only by a referendum. What is a referendum?

_____

_____

(e)   The right to form unions is mentioned in the passage. Give an example of the type
       of union to which the Constitution is referring, and give **TWO** functions that this
       union performs for its members.

       Example of union _____

       First function _____

       Second function _____

(f)   Briefly explain **ONE** reason why it is important for young people to know about
       the Irish Constitution (Bunreacht na hÉireann).

_____

_____

_____

3.   **Discrimination**
     The Irish Traveller Movement conducted a survey among Travellers recording the types
     of discrimination that Travellers experience when looking for service in shops, hotels and
     pubs. The following information highlights the results of this survey.

     Study the information given below and answer the questions that follow.

PUBS

88% said they went to a pub.

77% of these said they had been told to leave a pub by bar staff.

79% of these said they had been refused a drink.

71% of these said they had been refused 'because we were Travellers'.

HOTELS

61% said they had tried to book a hotel for an occasion.

76% of these said they had experienced problems.

47% of these said that it was 'because we were Travellers'.

45% of these said they were asked to leave or cancel their booking.

SHOPS

54% said they had been asked to leave a shop.

66% said they had experienced others being served before them.

60% said they had been 'made a show of' (embarrassed) in shops.

(a)   What percentage of Travellers who went to a pub said they had been refused a drink?

_____

(b)   What percentage of Travellers said they tried to book a hotel for an occasion?

_____

(c)   What percentage of Travellers said they had experienced others being served before them in shops?

_____

(d)   From the survey name **ONE** human right that some Travellers may have been denied.

Human right _____

(e) Travellers have a separate and different culture from settled people. Describe **TWO** ways that Traveller culture is different from the culture of settled people. **Your answer must be written from a human rights approach.**

First way _____

_____

Second way _____

_____

(f) Apart from Travellers, can you name a group of people who may have experienced discrimination? Describe how these people have been discriminated against, and then suggest **TWO** ways that this type of discrimination could be prevented.

Name of the group _____

How they may have experienced discrimination _____

_____

_____

Two ways to prevent this type of discrimination

First way _____

_____

Second way _____

_____

3. **Interdependence**

The following information on trainers (running shoes) is adapted from the Trócaire CSPE web site. Study the information carefully and answer the questions that follow.

Trainers (running shoes)

Made up of dozens of different man-made materials, my trainers were assembled in a Korean-owned factory in Indonesia. The leather for the upper came from Texan cows whose hides were sent for tanning in South Korea, where wages are not high. Tanning is the process in which the hides are turned into leather and can involve very strong chemicals.

The Indonesian women who made by €64 shoes earned €2 a day and worked in temperatures nearing 40 degrees Celsius.

Tiger Woods, the golfer, is sponsored by trainer manufacturer Nike. They pay him nearly €38 million a year to wear their emblem on his cap and jumper.

The price of a trainer is divided up between the main groups involved in its production and distribution in the following way:

Groups involved	Percentage take
Nike	33%
Shops	50%
Factories (owners/managers)	11.5%
Factories (workers)	0.5%

(a) Of the groups involved in the production and distribution of trainers, which one of these is getting:

the highest percentage take? _____

the lowest percentage take? _____

(b) Why do you think Nike are prepared to pay Tiger Woods nearly €38 million a year to wear its emblem on his cap and jumper?

_____

_____

_____

(c) The production of trainers is an example of global interdependence. Using information **ONLY** from the passage, explain what this means.

_____

_____

_____

(d) Nike is an example of a multinational company. What does this mean?

A multinational company is _____

_____

(e) Give an example of **TWO** different multinational industries working in Ireland, and give an example of what each produces.

Examples of multinational industries in Ireland.

Example 1 _____

This industry produces _____

Example 2 _____

This industry produces _____

(f) Multinational companies can be both good and bad for the development of a country. Describe **ONE** way in which these companies can be good for **and ONE** way that they can be bad for the development of a country.

One way that multinationals are good for the development of a country is

_____

_____

5

One way that multinationals are bad for the development of a country is

_____

_____

_____

Section 3
Answer ONE of the questions numbered 1, 2, 3, 4 below.

1. **Voting**

   You have discovered from a recent survey that many of the senior students in your school who are eligible to vote do not intend to vote in the next general election.

   (a) Write a short speech that your CSPE class will give to the senior students at a lunchtime meeting outlining at least **THREE** reasons why they should vote in the general election.

   (b) Draw a sketch of a poster that you would design to encourage them to attend this meeting. You should include an appropriate slogan in your sketch as well as an outline drawing or graphic.

   (c) (i) Suggest **TWO** reasons why some young people are not interested in voting.
       (ii) Suggest **ONE** way that they could be encouraged to vote.

2. **Refugees and asylum seekers**

   It is proposed to turn a hotel in your area into a reception centre for a group of refugees and asylum seekers.

   (a) Describe **TWO** actions that your CSPE class could take to make the children in this group feel welcome as students in your school.

   (b) Write a letter to an adult leader in this group inviting him/her to talk to your CSPE class. In your letter name **THREE** human rights issues affecting refugees in Ireland that the class would like to discuss with him/her. You should also clearly explain to the leader why you have been discussing these issues in your CSPE class.

(c) Write **THREE** questions that you would ask this leader about his/her experience as a refugee or asylum seeker **before** coming to Ireland. In each case give a reason for asking the question as part of your CSPE course.

3. **Vandalism**

There have been several incidents of vandalism at your school during school time, and your CSPE class wishes to do something to prevent it from happening again.

(a) You intend to carry out a survey in your school on this issue. Write **FIVE** questions that you would ask in this survey. Give a reason for asking each question in relation to the problem of vandalism.

(b) Write a short article for the school magazine explaining how the rights of students are affected when such vandalism occurs. In your answer you should mention at least **THREE** such rights.

(c) Describe **THREE** ways that the students in your school could become actively involved with the school management in preventing this type of vandalism from occurring again.

4. **A European Youth Parliament**

You have been invited to take part in a European Youth Parliament debate.

(a) Name **THREE** major political issues that you consider important to young European people today. In your answer explain why you think each of these political issues should be debated at the European Youth Parliament.

(b) In the case of **ONE** of these political issues, write a short speech that you would deliver to the Parliament outlining the importance of the issue. Include in your speech a **THREE**-point action plan that would help address this particular political issue in a meaningful way.

(c) Class councils, student councils and youth parliaments are often considered by adults to be a very good way of getting young people to become interested in politics. Do you agree with this statement? In your answer you must first state **either** YES I do agree with this statement **or** NO I do not agree with this statement. You should then explain you answer.

5

Please tick √ the question from Section 3 that you are answering.

Q. 1 ☐   Q. 2 ☐   Q. 3 ☐   Q. 4 ☐

Appendix

Useful addresses, e-mails and websites

▨ Non-Government Organisations

ACTIONAID Ireland
Unity Buildings
16-17 Lower O'Connell Street
Dublin 1
Tel: (01) 878 7911
www.actionaidireland.org

Christian Aid Ireland
Christ Church
Rathgar Road
Dublin 6
Tel: (01) 496 6184

Concern Worldwide
Camden Street
Dublin 2
Tel: (01) 475 4162 Fax: (01) 475 7362
E-mail: info@concern.ie
www.concern.ie

Goal
P.O. Box 19
Dun Laoghaire
Co. Dublin
Tel: (01) 280 9779
E-mail: info@goal.ie
www.goal.ie

Gorta
12 Herbert Street
Dublin 2
Tel: (01) 661 5522 Fax: (01) 661 2627
E-mail: admin@gorta.ie
www.gorta.ie

Irish Red Cross Society
16 Merrion Square
Dublin 2
Tel: (01) 676 5135 Fax: (01) 676 7171
www.redcross.ie

Oxfam in Ireland
19 Clanwilliam Terrace
Dublin 2
Tel: (01) 661 8544 Fax: (01) 661 8568
E-mail: oxireland@oxfam.ie
www.oxfam.ie

Trócaire
169 Booterstown Avenue
Blackrock
Co. Dublin
Tel: (01) 288 5385 Fax: (01) 288 3577
E-mail: info@trocaire.ie
www.trocaire.ie

A.F.r.I. (Action From Ireland)
Rathmines Road Lower,
Dublin 6.
Tel: (01) 496 8595

▨ Animal Welfare

Blue Cross Animal Welfare Society
8 Dartmouth Terrace
Ranelagh
Dublin 6
Tel: (01) 497 1985

Irish Society for the Prevention of Cruelty to Animals
300 Lower Rathmines Road
Dublin 6
Tel: (01) 497 7222 Fax: (01) 497 7940
E-mail: info@ispca.ie
www.ispca.ie

Irish Animals on the Web
E-mail: info@irishanimals.com
www.irishanimals.ie

Compassion in World Farming
Salmon Weir
Hanover Street
Cork
Co. Cork
Tel: (021) 272 1441
E-mail: ciwf@indigo.ie
www.ciwf.ie

Irish Horse Protection League
Aldave Manor
Kilbride
Blessington
Co. Wicklow
Tel: (01) 458 2460

WILD (Trust for the Welfare of Captive Wildlife)
P.O. Box 4827
Dublin
Tel: (01) 874 3925

Care of the Elderly

Age Action Ireland
Head Office
30 Lower Camden Street
Dublin 2
Tel: (01) 478 5060

ALONE
1 Willie Bermingham Place
Kilmainham Lane
Dublin 8
Tel: (01) 679 1032

Childrens's Welfare

Barnardos
Christchurch Square
Dublin 8
Tel: (01) 453 0355 Fax: (01) 453 0300
E-mail: info@barnardos.ie
www.barnardos.ie

Barretstown Gang Camp
Barretstown Castle
Ballymore Eustace
Co. Kildare
Tel: (045) 864115 Fax: (045) 864197
E-mail: info@barretstowngc.ie
www.barretstowngc.ie/

Irish National Committee for UNICEF
28 Lower Ormond Quay
Dublin 1
Tel: (01) 878 3000 Fax: (01) 878 6655
E-mail: unicefir@indigo.ie

Irish Society for the Prevention of Cruelty to Children
20 Molesworth Street
Dublin 2
Tel: (01) 679 4944 Fax: (01) 679 1746
E-mail: ispcc@ispcc.ie
www.ispcc.ie

Save the Children
15 Popper House,
Belfast BT10 0HB
Tel: (01232) 431123 Fax: (01232) 431314
E-mail: r.mcdonald@scfuk.org.uk

Chernobyl Children's Project
Camden Place
Camden Quay
Cork
Co. Cork
Tel: (021) 506411 Fax: (021) 551544
E-mail: adiroche@indigo.ie
www.aardvark.ie/ccp/contents.html

Employment and Emigration

Emigrant Advice
1a Catherdal Street
Dublin 1
Tel: (01) 873 2844

**Irish National Organisation of
the Unemployed**
Araby House
8 North Richmond Street
Dublin 1
Tel: (01) 856 0088
E-mail: inou@iol.ie

Environment

Conservation Volunteers Ireland
PO Box 3836
Ballsbridge
Dublin 4
Tel: (01) 668 1844

Earthwatch
(Friends of the Earth Ireland)
20 Grove Road
Rathmines
Dublin 6
Tel: (01) 497 3773 Fax: (01) 497 0412
E-mail: foeeire@iol.ie
www.iol.ie/~foeeire/home.htm

**ECO: Irish Environmental Conservation
Organisation for Youth - UNESCO Clubs**
39 Fleet Street
Dublin 2
Tel: (01) 679 9673

**ENFO - The Environmental Information
Service**
17 St Andrew's Street
Dublin 2
Tel: (01) 888 2001 Fax: (01) 888 2946
www.enfo.ie

VOICE
14 Upper Pembroke Street
Dublin 2
Tel: (01) 661 8123 Fax: (01) 661 8114
E-mail: avoice@iol.ie
www.voice.buz.org

An Taisce
Tailors' Hall
Back Lane
Dublin 8
E-mail: nsc@antaisce.org
www.antaisce.org

Burren Action Group
Clogher
Kilfenora
Co.Clare
Tel/Fax: (065) 708 8187
E-mail: burrenag@iol.ie
www.iol.ie/~burrenag/

Irish Peatland Conservation Council
119 Capel Street
Dublin 1
Tel: (01) 872 2384 Fax: (01) 872 2397
E-mail: ipcc@indigo.ie
www.ipcc.ie

Cork Environmental Alliance
34 Princes Street
Cork
Co. Cork
Tel: (021) 272277 Fax: (021) 274525
E-mail: cea@iol.ie
www.iol.ie/~cea

The Irish Wildlife Trust
170 Lower Baggot St.
Dublin 2
Tel: (01) 676 8588 Fax: (01) 676 8601
E-mail: enquiries@iwt.ie

European Union

European Commission
18 Dawson Street
Dublin 2
Tel: (01) 662 5113 Fax: (01) 662 5118

European Parliament Office in Ireland
43 Molesworth Street
Dublin 2
Tel: (01) 605 7900 Fax: (01) 605 7999
www.europarl.eu.int

EUROPA is the main server for EU information:
http://europa.eu.int

Fair Trade & Ethical Trade
(also see Aid Agencies)

Irish Fair Trade Network
17 Lower Camden Street
Dublin 2
Tel: (01) 475 3515

World Development Movement
25 Beehive Place
London SW9 7BR
England
www.wdm.org.uk

Fair Trade & Ethical Trade Websites

www.oneworld.org/
www.mcspotlight.org
www.essential.org/monitor/
www.fairtrade.org
www.gn.apc.org/babymilk
www.antislavery.org
www.rugmark.de/english

Homelessness

Focus Ireland
14a Eustace Street
Dublin 2
Tel: (01) 671 2555 Fax: (01) 679 6843
E-mail: focusirl@indigo.ie
www.focusireland.ie/

Trust
Bride Road
Dublin 8
Tel: (01) 671 2555 Fax: (01) 679 6843
E-mail: info@trust-ireland.ie
www.trust-ireland.ie

Simon Community
St Andrew's House
28 Exchequer Street
Dublin 2
Tel: (01) 671 1606 Fax: 671 1098
E-mail: simon@simoncommunity.com
www.simoncommunity.com

Human Rights
(also see Aid Agencies)

Amnesty International
48 Fleet Street
Dublin 2
Tel: (01) 677 6361
E-mail: info@amnesty.iol.ie
www.amnesty.ie

East Timor Campaign
24 Dame Street
Dublin 2
Tel: (01) 671 9207
E-mail: etisc@indigo.ie
www.freedom.tp/ireland/etisc

People with Disabilities

Irish Council for People with Disabilities
Con Colbert House
Inchicore Road
Dublin 8
Tel: (01) 473 2254 Fax: (01) 473 2262
E-mail: estgroup@iol.ie
www. fusio.ie

Irish Wheelchair Association
24 Blackheath Drive
Clontarf
Dublin 3
Tel: (01) 833 5366
www.iwa.ie

National Council for the Blind of Ireland
PV Doyle House
Whitworth Road
Dublin 9
Tel: (01) 830 7033

National Association for Deaf People
35 Nth Fredrich Street
Dublin 1
Tel: (01) 872 3800 Fax: (01) 872 3816
E-mail: nad@iol.ie
www.iol.ie/~nad/

Political Parties

Fianna Fáil
Aras de Valera
13 Upper Mount Street
Dublin 2
Tel: (01) 676 1551
E-mail: info@fiannafail.ie
www.fiannafail.ie

Fine Gael
51 Upper Mount Street
Dublin 2
Tel: (01) 676 1573
E-mail: finegael@finegael.com
www.finegael.ie

The Green Party
5A Upper Fownes Street
Dublin 2
Tel: (01) 679 0012
E-mail: greepar@iol.ie
www.greenparty.ie

The Labour Party
17 Ely Place
Dublin 2
Tel: (01) 661 2615
E-mail: head office@labour.ie
www.labour.ie

Progressive Democrats
25 South Frederick Street
Dublin 2
Tel: (01) 679 4399
E-mail: jackm@iol.ie
www.iol.ie/pd

Sinn Fein
44 Parnell Street
Dublin 1
Tel: (01) 872 6100
E-mail: sinnfein@iol.ie
www.sinnfein.ie

The Socialist Party
141 Thomas Street
Dublin 8
Tel: (01) 667 2686
E-mail: dublinsp@clubi.ie
www.socialistparty.net

Refugees

Association of Asylum Seekers and Refugees in Ireland (ARASI)
213 Nth Circular Road
Dublin 7
Tel: (01) 838 1142

Irish Refugee Council
35-36 Arran Quay
Dublin 7
Tel: (01) 872 4424 Fax: (01) 872 4411
E-mail: refugee@iol.ie
www.irishrefugeecouncil.ie

Refugee Trust
4 Dublin Road
Stillorgan
Co. Dublin
Tel: (01) 283 4256

SPECIFIC IRISH ORGANISATIONS

Combat Poverty Agency
Bridgewater Centre
Conyngham Road
Islandbridge
Dublin 8
Tel: (01) 670 6746

Irish Commission for Justice and Peace
169 Booterstown Avenue
Blackrock
Co. Dublin
Tel: (01) 288 5021

People in Need Trust
34 William Street South
Dublin 2
Tel: (01) 679 2944

Society of St Vincent de Paul
8 New Cabra Road
Dublin 7
Tel: (01) 838 4164

Travellers

Dublin Committee for Travelling People
St Catherine's Church
Meath Street
Dublin 8
Tel: (01) 454 6488

Pavee Point
46 North Great Charles Street
Dublin 1
Tel: (01) 878 0255 Fax: (01) 874 2626
E-mail: pavee@iol.ie
www.paveepoint.ie

■ United Nations

United Nations Headquarters
New York, NY 10017
USA
Tel: (001212) 963 1234:
www.un.org

United Nations Office
Palais des Nations
Switzerland
CH-1211 Geneva 10
Tel: (004122) 907 1234

United Nations Centre for Ireland
21st Floor
Millbank Tower
21-24 Millbank
London SW1P 4QH
England

■ Youth

National Youth Council of Ireland
3 Montague Street
Dublin 2
Tel: (01) 478 4122

Gaisce
The President's Award
State Apartments
Dublin Castle
Dublin 2
Tel: (01) 475 8746 Fax: (01) 475 8749
E-mail: mail@p-award.net
www.p-award.net

You can connect to many of these websites by visiting
the *Impact!* website at
www.gillmacmillan.ie/impact

Picture Credits

For permission to reproduce photographs and other material, the authors and publisher gratefully acknowledge the following:

AFP: 160 bottom.

ASSOCIATED PRESS: Sayyid Azim 171.

CORBIS: Jim Richardson 2, DiMaggio/Kalish 3, Little Blue Wolf Productions 9 top, Todd Gipstein 9 centre, Bernard and Catherine Desjeux 9 bottom, Jeremy Horner 12 left, Peter Turnley 12 centre, 47 right, 155 top, Lightscapes photography, Inc. 1 left/12 right, Farrell Grehan 20, Hulton-Deutsch Collection 23 top, David Turnley 23 centre and bottom, 24, 47 left, Ariel Skelley 1 bottom left/25 bottom, Strauss/Curbis 26, Geray Sweeney 1 top right/27 right, 27 left, 48, Flip Schulke 29 right, Tom and Dee Ann McCarthy 33 bottom, Bill Varie 35 bottom, Craig Aurness 38 top, Alan Towse; Ecoscene 38 bottom, Stephanie Maze 39 top, Macduff Everton 39 centre, Kelly-Mooney Photography 1 top centre/41, Paul Thompson; Eye Ubiquitous 53 top, Vittoriano Rastelli 71, Ian Harwood; Ecoscene 130 top, Photomorgana 145, Entymann Cyril/Corbis Sygma 147 top, Andrew Brookes 149, Franz-Marc Frei 151, Leif Skoogfors 152, 163 bottom, David Pollack 139 top centre/157, James Leynse/Corbis SABA 139 left/158, Yves Debay; The Military Picture Library 163 top, Bohan Brecelj 169, Gina Glover 180, Owen Franken 184, Gary Braasch 187.

DEREK SPEIRS: 13, 15, 16, 40, 51 left/53 middle, 52, 58 left, 51 centre/60, 86, 88, 90 centre, second from bottom, bottom/93, 91 centre, 83 left/96 top, 98, 83 centre/104, 83 bottom right/105 bottom, 108, 109, 119, 142 top, 150 left, 160 left, 182 bottom, 185 bottom, 233 all.

IMAGEFILE: Dan Couto 25, Pedro Coll 111.

INPHO: 155 bottom.

THE IRISH IMAGE COLLECTION: 17, 69, 114, 117 both, 118, 142 bottom.

POPPERFOTO: Reuters NewMedia Inc./Corbis 92, 139 right centre/160, second from left, centre, right, 172, 176, 177.

REX FEATURES: Martin McCullough 28 top, Nils Jorgensen 35 top, Isopress Senepart 90 top, Peter Macdiarmid 83 top right/91 top, Ron Sachs 103, MMC 105, Startraks 130 centre, Sutton-Hibbert 130 bottom, Rex 140, Vidal 147 bottom, Sipa Press 37, 148, 160 second from right, 174, 175, 178, Philip Moore 161 top, Ron Sachs 170, Kip Rano 86 left, Sinopix 86 right.

RUGMARK: Robin Romano 166, 167 both, 168.

OTHER PHOTOGRAPHS: 42 both courtesy of Galway City Council; 55 © Billy MacGill photos; 59 courtesy of Rice College, CBS, Ennis; 68 courtesy of Keith Heneghan; 73 right courtesy of Jason Clarke Photography; 73 left courtesy of Maxwell Picture Agency; 90 second from bottom courtesy of Fine Gael; 96 centre and bottom, 97 bottom and 120 courtesy of Oireachtas Broadcasting Unit; 112 bottom courtesy of An Garda Síochána; 126 bottom courtesy of Waterpoint, Enniscrone; 128 courtesy of AXIS Ballymun; 132